STUDY GUIDE & WORKBOOK

ANTHONY BRESCIA

*Revised and Updated
by*
PEGGY DYE

The Western Heritage
Brief Edition

Volume II: Since 1648
Third Edition

Donald Kagan
Yale University

Steven Ozment
Harvard University

Frank M. Turner
Yale University

Prentice Hall, Upper Saddle River, New Jersey 07458

© 2002, 1999, 1996 by PEARSON EDUCATION, INC.
Upper Saddle River, New Jersey 07458

ISBN 0-13-041598-7
Printed in the United States of America

Table of Contents

Introduction

WELCOME to the Brief Edition of the Guide. Users of this study tool will find the sections updated and corresponding to *The Western Heritage Brief Edition.*

Generally defined, history is learning about humankind's continuing experience by inquiry. It is the process of asking questions about things that have happened, are happening, and are likely to happen in the future. History deals with the essence of being human. It is one of the studies that most clearly separates the human species from all others. From the very beginning of human development peoples have asked, "What's happening?" Why have they done so? What is it about us that causes the questions to be asked? It is the human species, collectively, and each of us alone that has the capacity to think and reason beyond the present. To be human is to be historical. No other creature is endowed with the ability to consider time and space, what has gone before and what will come after. To understand civilization one must also contemplate death. You and I are among the only animals of the earth who early in life must come to grips with the inevitability of our own mortality. So that we may each better understand these realities the study of history has become the structured process that is organized to reflect the growth of civilizations and the development of their human cargo.

No matter what is said about the study of history, our understanding of the past remains the core of a liberal arts education, the mark of an educated person, and an essential adjunct to our lives, regardless of career choice. This is true because many of the methods used to learn about the past are similar to the skills we use to understand the present. We are, in fact, doing little more than very carefully and thoughtfully reading the newspaper of today's past. By so doing, and by drawing on the skills of the text writers, we are seeking an enlightened, manageable, and comprehensible view of what has been.

The study of history is both a joy and a discipline. It is a joy because it brings into our lives much of the fascinating past. Yet, because there is so much of that past available to us, historical research or study can be a chore, although it need not be.

This edition of the *Guide* is designed to serve students seeking a better understanding of their own heritage within that of the West. It can be used to improve one's grade and also one's overall study skills. Any student, whatever his or her ability, will benefit from the commentary and exercises provided. The *Guide* is another means by which your instructor, the authors of the textbook, and the authors of this workbook hope to guide you through this study of the past.

As noted below, the chapter-related exercises are designed to reinforce the historical ideas and thoughts presented within each chapter of the textbook. Attention is also called to historical persons and events that are essential to understanding the fabric of the past. Virtually all chapters include map exercises.

Designed as a supplement to the text, this volume can be used to gain an overall view of a particular chapter, and to call attention to selected items of historical importance within each chapter. The use of this *Guide* also provides an opportunity to test yourself on the material you have read in each chapter. These short-answer-type questions are of a kind commonly found and increasingly utilized at various levels of our educational system and in many subject areas. These questions are intended to sharpen your understanding of the chapter and to help in the comprehension of the historic data, whereas the essay questions are aimed at encouraging thought and an understanding of the larger concepts developed within each chapter. Map exercises are provided so that places and their importance in the historical picture are not lost. Continued attention has been given to physical geography in this edition. The *Guide* is arranged by chapters that correspond to those of the text. As in previous editions the page numbers corresponding to the textbook are appropriately provided throughout. Within each chapter of this *Guide* you will find the following:

Commentary

A brief overview that highlights the development of each chapter, this section is intended to present an overall understanding of the chapter. You should read this section for a preview and later as a review of the text material.

Identifications [Historical]

These are a selection of notable terms, places, events, and persons that are introduced in the chapter. *It should be noted that these identifications are only a selected sample.* They are designed to call your attention to those historical factors that are beyond the obvious and therefore appear to be of lesser importance. Use this section to deepen your understanding of specific items within each chapter.

Map Exercises

These exercises, marked A and B, are intended to familiarize you with the geography and the location of important places, events, and boundaries within a specific region or wider area. Some of these exercises will require you to consult other sources or an atlas.

Short-Answer Exercises

The multiple-choice, true/false, and completion questions are designed to help you check on specific points and ideas developed within the chapter. These questions are not intended to be difficult, and you should be able to answer them after a reasonably careful study of the chapter. The correct answers are provided at the end of each chapter, along with the appropriate page references to *The Western Heritage Brief*.

For Further Consideration

These essay questions are aimed at provoking thought about the wider concepts and historical problems raised within each chapter, BUT are generally different than those found at the end of each chapter of the text itself.

13
Paths to Constitutionalism and Absolutism:
England and France in the Seventeenth Century

Commentary

Nearly a century of constitutional crises shook England after Elizabeth's reign. The core of the conflict was a power struggle between Parliament and the Stuart kings—in succession, James I, Charles II, and James II. The kings and Parliament struggled over taxes and religion. The kings sought ways to tax or otherwise raise money—from grants, loans, or other sources—by bypassing the approval of Parliament. Parliament's main power lay in levying taxes. Religion also fed the conflict. The kings leaned so heavily toward imposing an "Anglo-Catholicism" on their subjects that they collided with the Protestant Puritans dominating Parliament.

The escalating social skirmishes led finally to open civil war and the "Glorious Revolution." The Glorious Revolution established several changes that would set England's government system for centuries to come—indeed, to the present. Changes included a Bill of Rights guaranteeing the civil liberties of England's privileged classes. The monarch's rule became subject to law and to Parliament's consent. Roman Catholics were also prohibited from occupying the throne. The new system found its philosophical justification in John Locke's *Second Treatise of Government*. Along the way to this end of the civil wars were other milestones. One of the most important came when Oliver Cromwell's army conquered Ireland and Scotland, unifying what we know today as Great Britain.

The path of events itself took many twists and turns. During the reign of James I and his son Charles I, the conflict between king and Parliament escalated. Then, in what contributed to his downfall, Charles I tried to impose English religious conformity on England and Scotland, that is, Anglo-Catholicism. Scotland revolted, English Puritans in Parliament also were roused, and civil war broke out in 1642. Ultimately the fanatical Puritan army of Oliver Cromwell won. Cromwell executed the king and abolished the monarchy and the House of Lords and the Anglican church. Civil war had become revolution. But Cromwell's harsh rule, expensive wars, inattention to commerce, and fanatical morals pushed the Parliament to invite the son of Charles I to take the throne back after Cromwell died. This is called the "Stuart Restoration." But in a final twist, Charles II's successor, brother James II, tried to make his royal power absolute and also made his Catholic sympathies clear. So Parliament brought in the army of James' son-in-law and daughter, the Protestant William of Orange (Netherlands) and Mary. James was deposed, and the Glorious Revolution succeeded in 1688.

By comparison, France moved not through bloody civil wars and towards relative democracy but towards royal absolutism and religious persecution. Henry IV, in the early 1600s, reined in the privileges of the French nobility. His finance minister Sully expanded governmental authority, establishing royal monopolies on gunpowder, salt, and mines. Sully began construction of a canal system and drafted workers to build and maintain roads. Such policies expanded under Henry's successors, Louis XIII and Louis XIV. Their chief ministers were the brilliant and Machiavellian Cardinals Richelieu and Mazarin. The Cardinals and Louis XIV, in particular, perfected strategies to ensure an absolutist king. In 1649, the

French nobles revolted in a series of rebellions including popular support. The rebellions were called the Fronde, and after near-anarchy resulted by 1652, popular support shifted to want a king and strong order. Louis XIV took advantage, including becoming a master propagandist, continuously reminding the populace of the grandeur of the crown, and he also sought ways to make the nobility dependent on his power and trivial in their own. He built Versailles, an unprecedented royal expense—costing half the royal income. Versailles kept many nobles busy in elaborate rituals and amusing distractions while the real business of government was handled by Louis' trusted advisors who also depended on his power. Louis pursued wars of expansion, possessing the largest European army. Louis also crushed religious dissent, whether among Catholics like the mystical Jansenists, or among Protestants like the Huguenots. One of the king's most harsh acts was to revoke the Edict of Nantes of 1658 which had established a legal Protestant minority in Catholic France. After Louis' revocation, Protestant churches and schools closed, clergy was exiled, and the laity was enslaved on the galleys. The royal income to afford the far-reaching kingly ambitions came mainly from the peasantry in the form of the *taille*, a direct tax. Finally, the war that broke French supremacy was the War of the Spanish Succession, which lasted 14 years until 1714, enveloping all of western Europe, engaging England too, and stirring tax revolts in France and terrible carnage. The seventeenth century had belonged to France, especially to Louis XIV, the "Sun King," but England would have the eighteenth century.

Identifications

Identify each one of the following as used in the text. Refer to the text as necessary.

	Text page
impositions	242
Duke of Buckingham	243, 244
Petition of Right	244
policy of thorough	244
Short Parliament and John Pym	244
Grand Remonstrance	245
Cavaliers and Roundheads	245
"Pride's Purge"	245
Clarendon Code and the New Model Army	247
English Bill of Rights of 1689	247
Toleration Act of 1689	247
Louis XIV's saying, "one king, one law, one faith"	248
intendants	249
Fronde	249, 250
Edict of Nantes	249, 250
Bishop Bossuet and "Gallican Liberties"	250
Blaise Pascal and Jansenism	253
mercantilism	253
taille	253
Sebastien Vauban and Marquis of Louvois	253
Battle of Malplaquet	257
Peace of Utrecht-Rastadt	257

Map Exercise A

Locate each of the following areas on the accompanying map:

1. Normandy
2. English Channel
3. North Sea
4. Atlantic Ocean
5. River Seine
6. Aix-la-Chapelle
7. the Hague
8. Paris
9. Versailles
10. Nantes
11. Brussels
12. Utrecht
13. Amsterdam
14. Flanders
15. Avignon
16. Cambridge
17. London
18. Ireland

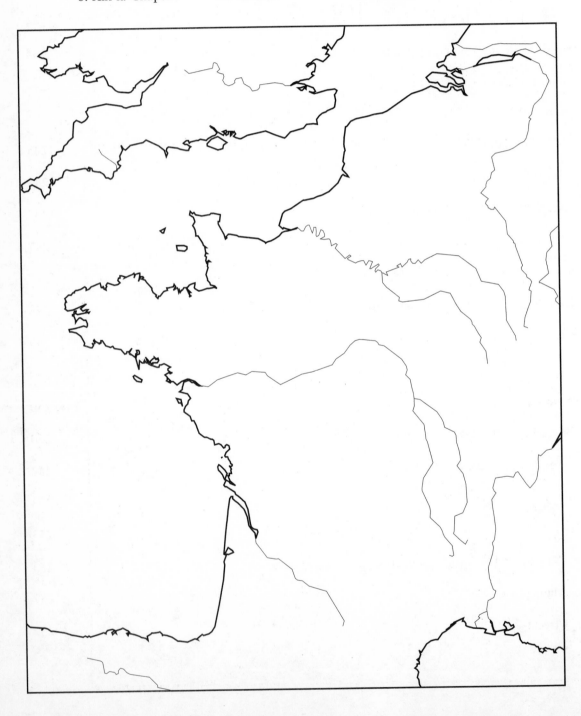

Map Exercise B

Doing your own research, on this map of France, locate and mark each of the following areas and cities:

RIVERS: Garonne, Loire, Rhone, Seine

MOUNTAINS: Central Massif, Pyrenees, Vosges

WATERS: Bay of Biscay, English Channel, Mediterranean Sea

CITIES: Bordeaux, Cherbourg, La Rochelle, Le Havre, Lyons, Marseilles, Nantes, Orleans, Paris, Tours

Useful Internet sites include that of this text:
http://www.prenhall.com/kagan

and that of the University of Texas:
http://www.lib.utexas.edu/LIBS/PCL/map_collection/france.html

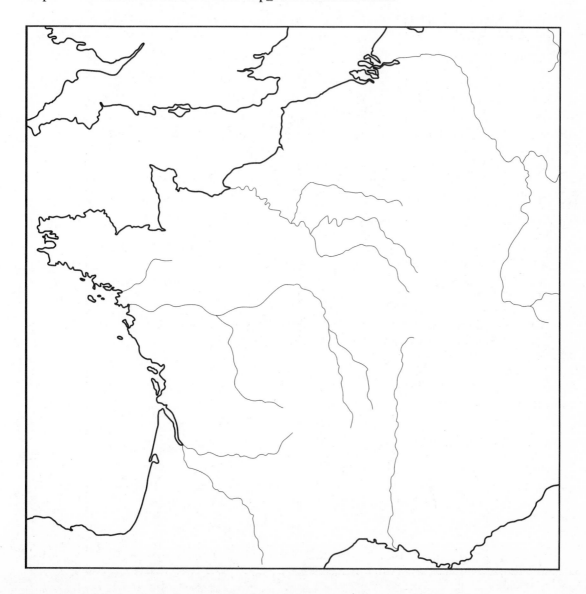

Short-Answer Exercises

Multiple-Choice

_____1. The book *A Trew Law of Free Monarchies* was written to advocate the divine right of kings to rule and the author was:
   (a) James VI of Scotland
   (b) John Locke
   (c) Charles I
   (d) Oliver Cromwell

_____2. Disappointment and disgust with James I over his lavish lifestyle, sale of peerages, and religious liberalism—allowing games on Sundays—led Puritans to:
   (a) start England's first traveling tent-revival meetings
   (b) leave England to found Massachusetts Bay Colony
   (c) campaign for the public flogging of the king's rumored lover, the Duke of Buckingham
   (d) none of the above

_____3. Which of the following was least supportive of English monarchial government in the period 1620 through the 1640s?
   (a) Duke of Buckingham
   (b) John Pym
   (c) Thomas Wentworth
   (d) William Laud

_____4. Among the fears and grievances which the British Parliament had with Charles II were:
   (a) Charles' "forced loayns" from people with property
   (b) Charles' billetting troops in private homes
   (c) Charles' selling titles of nobility
   (d) all of the above

_____5. The reason for the continuing opposition to the reign of James II was his:
   (a) imprisonment of Anglican bishops
   (b) appointments of known Catholics to high offices
   (c) insistence upon the repeal of the Test Act
   (d) all of these

_____6. Which of the following was least directly responsible for the establishment of absolutism in France during the seventeenth century?
   (a) Louis XIII
   (b) Sully
   (c) Richelieu
   (d) Mazarin

_____7. Jansenists believed that:
   (a) human beings had been redeemed through Christ's death
   (b) Cornelis Jansen should be canonized
   (c) that human beings could not be redeemed without special grace from God
   (d) St. Augustine had incorrectly interpreted the concept of original sin

_____8. The marquis of Louvois is noted for all of the following except:
 (a) establishing a professional French army
 (b) developing a system of trench warfare
 (c) introducing a merit-based system of promotion
 (d) increasing army pay

_____9. Louis XIV considered the revocation of the Edict of Nantes as:
 (a) unimportant
 (b) militarily significant
 (c) his most pious act
 (d) good for business

_____10. Louis XIV created Versailles and an elaborate life at court there for his important nobles to:
 (a) protect them from uprisings in Protestant towns
 (b) keep them too busy to plot revolts
 (c) borrow from them to build copies of Versailles elsewhere, to be France's earliest resorts
 (d) none of the above

True/False

_____1. When rebellion broke out in Ireland in 1641, John Pym led Parliament's opposition to funding an army for the king, saying Parliament should take command of the army itself.

_____2. The alliance with Scottish Presbyterians and the reorganization of the army under Parliament assured the Puritan victory over Charles I.

_____3. Charles II of England, facing Parliament's resistance to grant him money, raised cash by increasing customs duties and getting aid from Louis XIV.

_____4. The English Toleration Act of 1689 granted religious freedom to all but the most radical religious groups.

_____5. Despite his persecution of the Huguenots at home, Cardinal Richelieu allied France with Swedish Protestants during the Thirty Years' War.

_____6. Throughout the seventeenth century, Catholic Jansenists allied with the Jesuits against French Huguenots.

_____7. Jean-Baptiste Colbert's economic policies had the effect of diminishing France's industrial and commercial potential.

_____8. Louis XIV's revocation of the Edict of Nantes did not harm Protestants beyond closing their churches.

_____9. Louis XIV's last war to try to win dominance over Europe, the War of the Spanish Succession, continued through famines and revolts against war taxes, and the war enveloped all of western Europe.

_____10. From a military perspective England's success in the War of Spanish Succession was the result of excellent leadership and superior weapons.

_____11. "L'etat c'est moi" ("I am the state") was Louis XIV's way of saying that the king answered to no one but God and that everyone else answered to him.

Completion

1. James VI of Scotland, who became James I of England, was the son of _____ .

2. The religious minister under Charles I was _____, and in the 1630s he provoked a war with Scotland.

3. The largest military engagement of the English Civil War was the 1644 battle at _____ .

4. The fate of Charles I appears to have been sealed when Cromwell's New Model Army defeated him at _____ in June 1645.

5. _____ was the official title used by Oliver Cromwell after taking power in 1653.

6. The so-called "Glorious Revolution" in England was justified in the work titled *Second Treatise on Government* written by _____ .

7. Primarily to build and maintain roads, an involuntary labor force was created in France in the seventeenth century by the introduction of the _____ .

8. Connecting the image of God to kings would be found in the writings of _____ .

9. The most famous of the defenders of the Jansenist movement was _____ .

10. _____ is the name used to describe the financial policies of the French minister Colbert.

11. The _____ was the direct tax on the peasants that provided much of the royal income to Louis XIII and Louis XIV.

12. The _____ was a series of popular rebellions, also involving the Parliament of Paris and discontented French nobles who tried to reverse the drive by Louis XIV towards absolute monarchy.

For Further Consideration

1. In seventeenth-century England, Parliament and the Stuart kings competed for political power, and religious issues played into their struggles. Look back to the reign of Elizabeth I, a hundred years before. What political and religious conflicts set the stage for the larger civil wars of the Stuart era?

2. Imagine that you are living in London just as "Lord Protector" Oliver Cromwell died and, with him, his military dictatorship. You are writing to your brother in the Massachusetts colony in America. He wants to know what led to the success of Cromwell's Puritans. Write him a list of at least four factors. Then write one failure that contributed to the restoration of the Stuart monarchy.

3. France in the seventeenth century became an absolute monarchy. Write one or two of the leading contributions made by Cardinals Richelieu and Mazarin and by Louis XIII and Louis XIV to create such power.

4. If you were writing an obituary on King Louis XIV, what would you say his reign accomplished? Where did it fall short? You may write from your own viewpoint as an historian, or write as a member of Louis' court in Versailles, or write as a Huguenot persecuted by the king or a peasant taxed for war.

5. Compare and contrast how the governments of England and France developed in the 1600s. What was one major change in each country's government? What was the main struggle in the process? Between whom? What laws or evidence shows the development? What was similar in both countries? Different?

or

Imagine that you write headlines for the British press. Write at least five that tell the biggest changes in the government from 1603 to 1688. Now cross the English Channel and write headlines about French government changes for the same period. Compare France and England. How have their governments developed similarly? Differently?

6. French finance minister Sully "dreamed of joining the whole of Europe into a kind of common market," says the text on page 249. What projects did Sully develop to fulfill his dream? What did Minister Colbert add? If you like, add your opinion on what these projects have in common with projects you know in today's global market.

7. (Optional) Looking over the seventeenth century, what role do you see religion playing in bringing communities together? In dividing them? Focus by using two examples. Pick any country you like from areas surveyed so far in Europe or the Americas.

Answers

Multiple-Choice

		Text page
1.	A	.242
2.	B	.243
3.	B	.244-245
4.	D	.244
5.	D	.247-248
6.	A	.242
7.	C	.251, 253
8.	B	.253-254
9.	C	.254
10.	B	.250

True/False

1.	T	.245
2.	T	.245
3.	T	.247
4.	F	.248
5.	T	.249
6.	F	.251, 253
7.	F	.253
8.	F	.254
9.	T	.256-257
10.	T	.256
11.	T	.250

Completion

1.	Mary Stuart, Queen of Scots	.242
2.	William Laud	.244
3.	Marston Moor	.245
4.	Naseby	.245
5.	Lord Protector	.246
6.	John Locke	.248
7.	*corveé*	.249
8.	Bishop Bossuet	.250
9.	Blaise Pascal	.253
10.	Mercantilism	.253
11.	*taille*	.253
12.	*Fronde*	.249

14

New Directions in Thought and Culture in the Sixteenth and Seventeenth Centuries

Commentary

During the sixteenth and seventeenth centuries, scientific breakthroughs created a new view of the universe that challenged traditional beliefs. The view of the Earth moved from the medieval assumption of being in the center of things to become merely one of several planets orbiting the sun. The sun itself became one of many stars. The new discoveries pushed European society to rethink humanity's place in the larger picture. "What is a man?" asked Hamlet and then answered himself in a short speech in a new play of 1603 by William Shakespeare. Traditional religion and the new discoveries came into conflict. An enthusiasm for nature as a machine—even as a giant clock ticking forward—challenged the medieval Scholastic emphasis on past achievements and obedience to authority. The scientific discoveries also joined other destabilizers of society in a long list. For instance: the Reformation, conquest in the Americas, booty and trade and industrial expansion for Europe's merchants, civil wars and revolution in England, a rebellious *Fronde* in France and then the rise of French absolutism, religious wars ranging from the Christians finally driving the Moors and Turks from Europe, to the Christians devastating each other in the Thirty Years' War and wiping out a third of Germany's population. Integrating all of this and the new science would drive European society to zigzag forward and back, raising questions which still influence Western culture.

To begin with science, astronomers led the discoveries, as mentioned, by seeing that the Earth revolved around the sun. Men calling themselves "natural philosophers," and including Nicolaus Copernicus, Johannes Kepler, and Galileo Galilei, pioneered such study. The new intellectuals were no lone actors, however. Opticians, metal workers, lawyers, sailors, and other artisans and craftspeople supplied tools and skills essential to the discoveries, and the natural philosophers came from all over Europe, being German, Dutch, Italian, English, and French. "Learned societies" sprung up to enable collaborations.

Looking even more closely, astronomers Copernicus, Brahe, Kepler, and Galileo applied mathematical reasoning to their studies. Galileo also used the newly invented telescope to verify Copernicus' sun-centered universe. The astronomers raised questions about the movement of the planets, as well—questions which, when Sir Isaac Newton solved them, laid a basis for modern physics. The new approach from astronomy also suggested mathematical models for beauty, social relationships, and political systems. Mathematician Rene Descartes proposed a method for finding truth by assuming doubt. The lawyer Sir Francis Bacon advocated a direct examination of nature to decide reality by empirical evidence and not by the Scholastic approach. Scholasticism presumed that most truth had already been discovered and only needed to be explained, not challenged.

Political philosophers adopted the new methods. Thomas Hobbes and John Locke examined human nature and the origin of state authority. Both men came out of the civil wars and period of revolution in England. Hobbes saw a dark, egotistical tendency in human nature and believed the threat of anarchy was worse than tyranny. He advocated a state tightly ruled by law and order. Locke, the most influential critic of Hobbes, had sympathies with popular revolution. He saw human nature to include goodwill and cooperation. He proposed that government be instituted to protect the liberty of human nature and not restrain it. Hobbes' and Locke's contrasting views have influenced political development in the West down to the present.

The new sense of a mathematical universe challenged religious beliefs and institutions. Blaise Pascal, a mathematician and physical scientist and deeply religious man, was one of the thinkers who tried to reconcile science and faith. Drawing on earlier, relatively conservative views of John Calvin and St. Augustine, he argued that only religion and faith could disclose the meaning of human nature. During this age, the Catholic Church condemned the Copernican view of the universe as unbiblical. Galileo was forced to repudiate his theories and lived his last years under house arrest. The Inquisition was active, and witch panics and devil hunting grew to the point where 70,000–100,000 people were sentenced to death between 1400 and 1700. Such panics came in part not only from religion, but from wars, and other divisions, destabilizing society. The weak were scapegoated.

Most of the victims of witch hunts were women. Women doing certain kinds of work, such as midwifery and nursing, found themselves particularly threatened. Unconventional women, women who did not marry and older women were targeted. Women also faced other, less deadly challenges all through this age of scientific innovation. Patriarchical traditions blocked women from the scientific societies, universities, and most of the new scientific work. Men claimed science. A few token exceptions included Margaret Cavendish, Duchess of Newcastle, who was introduced by her husband into natural philosophy. Among her scientific writings, she wrote a text intended to bring other women to the study of science. It was called *Description of a New World, Called the Blazing World* (1666). Artisan women had more opportunities than others to pursue science, since they trained to work in family businesses. Several German astronomers were assisted by wives and daughters, notably Maria Winkelman, who discovered a comet in 1702. After her husband died, however, she ultimately was forced to abandon astronomy.

The age was full of paradoxes, with steps forward and back. But society, in rethinking humanity's place in the scheme of things, developed questions and momentum that would give continuing life to Western inventions for centuries ahead.

Identifications

Identify each one of the following as used in the text. Refer to text as necessary.

Map Exercise A

Mark each of the known planets in its correct orbit on the Copernican model of the universe below. Do your own research. Possibly helpful Internet sites include that of this text:

http://www.prenhall.com/kagan

or the astronomy site:

http://www.onlineastronomy.com/astr161/retrograde/copernican.html

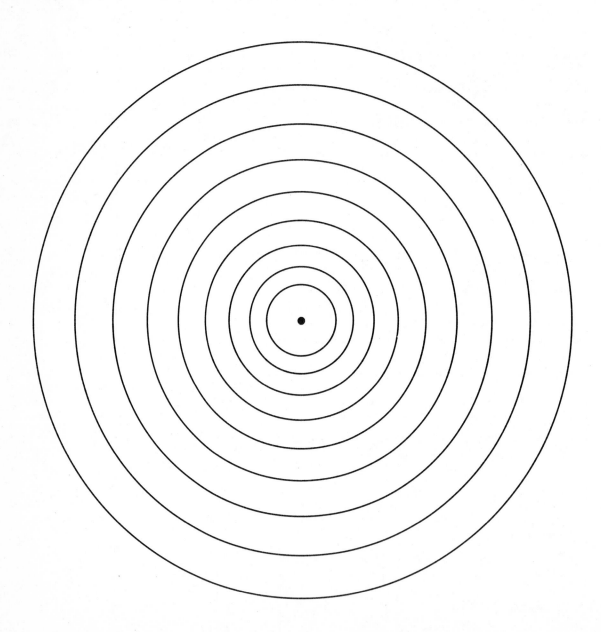

Map Exercise B

Tycho Brahe's (Naked-Eye) Astronomy

Following the empirical method described by Francis Bacon, repeat Tycho Brahe's experiment:

Observe the evening or early morning sky with your naked eye. Do you see the moon, sun, stars, haze, something else? Draw or make a map, or describe in words at least three of your observation. Collecting observations is in itself the goal. How does this method of collecting observations compare to studying history?

Short-Answer Exercises

Multiple-Choice

_____1. Which of the following expressions best characterizes the nature of the Scientific Revolution?
(a) it occurred in several places in Europe at the same time
(b) it was not revolutionary in the normal sense of the word
(c) it grew out of the criticism associated with the Reformation
(d) all of these are correct

_____2. Who failed to refute Copernicus' idea that the Earth revolved around the sun but succeeded in collecting the most accurate astronomical data ever caught by the naked eye?
(a) Tycho Brahe
(b) Johannes Kepler
(c) Galileo Galilei
(d) Francis Bacon

_____3. The new natural philosophy looked at Scholastic views of God by:
(a) challenging the idea that understanding nature would reveal divine mysteries
(b) attacking reverence for authority
(c) both a and b
(d) neither a nor b

_____4. Physics, the study of the laws of motion, found a new way to proceed when Galileo asked this question:
(a) why do objects change from a natural state of rest?
(b) does the sun ever stop moving?
(c) why do objects change at all—either from moving or resting?
(d) why do objects fall to the ground?

_____5. In seventeenth-century Europe, women endured:
(a) exclusion from universities and scientific societies
(b) witch hunts
(c) "scientific" arguments that men's brains were superior
(d) all of the above

_____6. Descartes, who invented analytic geometry, tried to:
(a) prove that the world was round
(b) challenge the church to prove that a holy heaven existed
(c) find the way to all truths by beginning with doubt
(d) none of the above

_____7. Pascal believed that:
(a) reason could reveal what faith in God could not
(b) misery loves company
(c) God sent material wealth to those who performed good works
(d) it is better to believe in God than not to

_____8. A main goal for "natural philosophers" (scientists) as advocated by Francis Bacon is to:
(a) pursue science not to improve human life but to find pure truth
(b) prove that most truth has already been discovered
(c) do one's own direct experiments to find a new understanding of nature

_____9. In Thomas Hobbes' view, man was:
    (a) a person neither good nor evil
    (b) a self-centered beast
    (c) essentially God-fearing

_____10. *Don Quixote* by Cervantes and Shakespeare's plays appeared in the seventeenth century, so students could enjoy them along with the new science in:
    (a) *Essay Concerning Human Understanding* by John Locke
    (b) *Frankenstein* by Isaac Newton
    (c) *Royal Society Witches* by Margaret Cavendish

True/False

_____1. Nicolaus Copernicus found the Ptolemaic system of the universe to be full of mathematical problems.

_____2. Eliminating women who did not submit to male control was one reason for witch hunts in the sixteenth century's patriarchal society.

_____3. The Catholic church promoted fear of demons, witches, and the Devil to maintain its claim to be the sole possessor of magic power.

_____4. Scientific advances and theories of a reasonable universe grew over the same period of 1400–1700 as did the witch hunts that killed 70,000–100,000 people, mostly women.

_____5. Although women were banned from science, a few were helped by men in their families to popularize scientific theories or to assist men who were natural philosophers.

_____6. The Englishman Francis Bacon is considered to be the founder of empiricism and experimentation in science.

_____7. In 1632, René Descartes wrote *Dialogues on the Two Chief Systems of the World*.

_____8. The Jansenists believed in the total sinfulness of humans, and their dependence on grace for salvation.

_____9. The English Civil War occurred during Thomas Hobbes' life, but he knew little about it because his family fled to Spain.

_____10. Thomas Hobbes supported the idea of a strong and efficient ruler because he believed such a ruler would alleviate the dangers for humans existing in the state of nature.

Completion

1. The Ptolemaic view of the universe is found in a work written in the second century and titled the _____ .

2. The work of _____ expanded on the previous efforts of Nicolaus Copernicus and Tycho Brahe.

3. For Galileo the rationality for the entire universe was based on _____ .

4. The pioneering thinkers of the sixteenth and seventeenth centuries did not call themselves scientists since the word "scientist" was not invented until the 1830s; instead they called themselves _____.

5. Intellectuals learned by meeting socially; for instance, Thomas Hobbes visited Paris and met _____ and spent time in Italy with Galileo.

6. The Catholic Church condemned the Copernican view of the universe, and forced _____ to repudiate his support of the Copernican view and endure nine years of house arrest.

7. One country in the center of intellectual developments in the 1500s and 1600s, with its opticians and metal workers producing the instruments for the new science, was _____.

8. The political philosopher Thomas Hobbes believed that, as far as government went, the dangers of _____ were greater than the dangers of tyranny.

9. Dutch artist _____ painted geographers and astronomers, using maps and globes, showing the practicalities and spirit of the age of exploration on Earth and in the heavens.

10. _____ believed that human ruling went beyond control of the jungle of selfish egomaniacs; it required the ruler to preserve the law of nature.

For Further Consideration

1. Describe the roles of Nicolaus Copernicus and Francis Bacon in influencing what is now referred to as the Scientific Revolution.

2. What was the new world view worked out during this era? How did it differ from the medieval view? What effects did the new concept of the universe have on all of the sciences?

3. In the Scientific Revolution, who, besides the intellectual elites, provided special skills and experience essential for the discoveries? How did people pursue their research? For example, what were learned societies? What role would you enjoy playing if you lived then?

4. What blocked women from playing a greater part in the development of the new science? What enabled some women, such as Margaret Cavendish, to work in the field? What do you see to be similar or different today?

5. How did Thomas Hobbes see human nature? How did John Locke? If you like, try writing as if from Hobbes' and Locke's own pen (or computer).

Answers

Multiple-Choice

		Text page
1.	D	260-261
2.	A	262
3.	C	264
4.	A	263
5.	D	267, 271, 268
6.	C	264-265
7.	D	268-269
8.	C	264
9.	B	265
10.	A	221-222, 263, 266, 268

True/False

1.	T	261
2.	T	271
3.	T	271
4.	F	269
5.	T	268
6.	T	264
7.	F	268
8.	T	269
9.	F	265
10.	T	265

Completion

1.	Almagest	261
2.	Johannes Kepler	262
3.	mathematics	262
4.	natural philosophers	261
5.	Descartes	265
6.	Galileo	268
7.	The Netherlands	270
8.	anarchy	265
9.	Vermeer	270
10.	John Locke	266

15

Successful and Unsuccessful Paths to Power (1686–1740)

Commentary

The end of the seventeenth and the early part of the eighteenth century was a period of state building. While perhaps not in the modern sense of nation building, wherein the role of the ordinary citizen would become a factor, it was in the sense of building the state organizational structure. The role of an increasingly international economy and empire building in the Americas contributed to the necessity of new infrastructures. The Reformation itself, the religiously inspired warfare that followed, and such great wars as the Thirty Years' War (1618–1648) and the Great Northern War (1700–1721) clearly undermined the medieval nature of state systems. The achievements of the Scientific Revolution also profoundly altered approaches to how states might be governed.

The most powerful states became those who developed strong central governments. The ways could vary somewhat. By the early eighteenth century, England worked with a Parliament of the propertied classes. Parliament, rather than the crown, controlled the army. This government also allowed more freedom as a whole for the majority of people. Newspapers and public debate flourished, and free speech and freedom of association were permitted. Corruption also was the glue that held the overall system—in this Age of (Prime Minister Robert) Walpole—together. England thus moved along the road of relative liberalism that would spur future industrial growth. In Brandenburg-Prussia (the future Germany) and in the Russia of Peter the Great, by contrast, the power of the state grew, not to control the army but to build the government around the military. In Prussia—the thirteenth largest population in Europe—the army was the third or fourth largest.

In France, the absolutism established under Louis XIV held up against resistance by weak-willed aristocrats and the church. Louis XV himself lacked leadership, becoming a pawn of court intrigues and scandalous living. The state's finances grew unstable, but France continued on with a centralized administration, a major military, and rich private commerce from colonies who spurred European industry.

To the east, continuing challenges met efforts by the Hapsburg emperor of Austria, Charles VI, to unify scattered lands of different languages and customs. Charles failed to produce a male heir, and his heiress daughter had her empire attacked by Prussia in a struggle that was to last for another century. In contrast to Austria, other nations developed modern state systems largely through the dominating personalities of monarchs and the military administrations they created. Such monarchs included Frederick William, the Great Elector of Prussia from the Hohenzollern family; his son Frederick William I; and Peter the Great of Russia. A major gain for Russia was its winning a port to Europe in war at Sweden's expense, breaking Sweden's dominance of the Baltic. Peter built St. Petersburg, inspired by Versailles, and provoked hostility on the part of some Russians who rejected European ways. Russia continued in conflict over Westernization for three centuries until 1917 and revolution.

Success and then downturn met the Netherlands which, in the 1600s, thrived as a republic, rising on the power of its commerce, shipbuilding, and finance. The Netherlands boasted the most advanced financial system of the century. But after 1702, its naval supremacy passed to England, its fishing industry declined, and the Dutch lost their lead in shipbuilding as well. They lacked a vigorous political leadership to confront these challenges. Although the country lost footing as a political power, it continued as a strong banking and stock exchange.

Decline also affected Spain—mentioned here but discussed in Chapter 12. Spain suffered humiliating defeat under France in a war stretching from the tail of the Thirty Years' War (i.e., from 1648 to 1659). The Treaty of the Pyrenees left Spain humbled. Spain also lost the Netherlands in their revolt and victory for independence between 1572 and 1648. Other declines came to Sweden, Poland, and the Ottoman Empire, which in various ways suffered from weak central governments or economies, including nobles able to resist and obstruct their rulers.

In international affairs, two long-term wars occurred. In central Europe, Austria and Prussia fought over leadership of Germany. In western Europe, France and Great Britain fought on two fronts—for domination over Europe and for control of overseas commerce. But economic and social changes ran alongside the wars. These changes would transform Europe far beyond the effects of military might in the era to come.

Identifications

Identify each one of the following as used in the text. Refer to the text as necessary.

	Text page
Dutch Republic and States General	275
William III, of the House of Orange	275
Dutch East Indies Company	276
The Mississippi Bubble	276
parlements	276
Tories and Whigs	278
South Sea Company	279
"Let sleeping dogs lie"	279
Robert Walpole and English ministerial cabinet	279
Bank of England	279
Parliament-House of Commons	279
"exploding" the Diet	281
Ottoman Empire's besieging Vienna	281
Treaty of Westphalia	281
Pragmatic Sanction	283
Prussian as an adjective	283
The Great Elector and the Junkers	284
Frederick William I	284
Russian "Time of Troubles"	285
Mikhail Romanov	285
boyers and *streltsy*	285-286
Table of Ranks	286
Old Believers Movement	286
Procurator General	286
Saint Petersburg	287

Map Exercise A

1. Locate the Adriatic Sea, and locate and mark the boundaries of states bordering the Austrian Empire. Useful maps may be found on pp. 239 and 282.

2. Trace the Danube River through the Austrian Empire.

3. Locate each of the following cities:

1. Vienna	4. Lemberg
2. Budapest	5. Belgrade
3. Prague	6. Mohacs

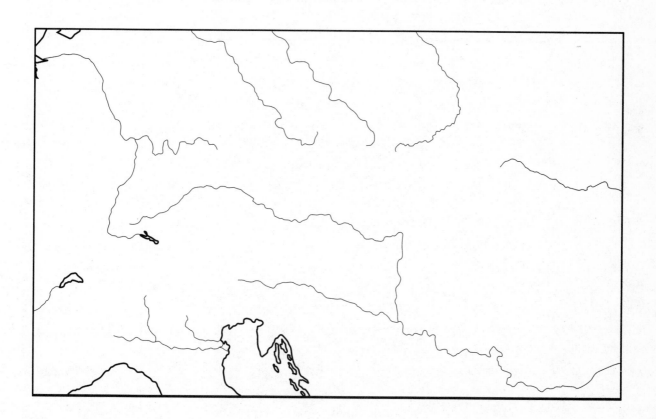

Map Exercise B

1. Outline each of the following countries/areas: Sweden, Finland, and Russia.

2. Locate the cities of Stockholm, St. Petersburg, Moscow, and Helsinki.

3. Mark the Baltic Sea, Lake Ladoga, and the Gulf of Finland.

Useful maps may be found on page 239 in your text and on the Internet site of your text:

http://www.prenhall.com/kagan

and a combined site of Stanford-University of Texas (using maps of the Central Intelligence Agency):

http://www.lib.utexas.edu/Libs/PCL/Map_collection/commonwealth/Russia94.jpg

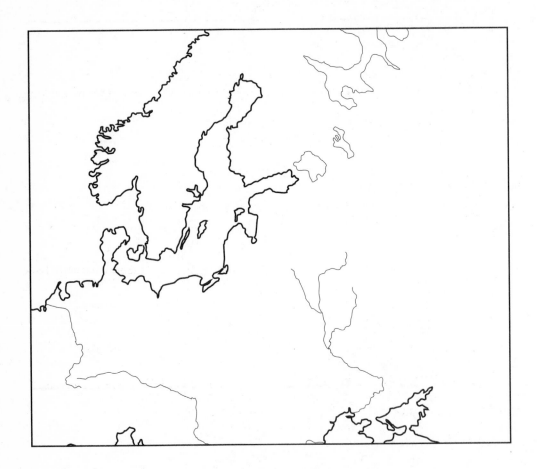

Short-Answer Exercises

Multiple-Choice

_____ 1. According to the text, which of the following countries was not moving forward in this period?
    (a) Great Britain
    (b) Russia
    (c) Spain
    (d) Prussia

_____2. Which of the following contributed *least* to the decline of the Netherlands in the eighteenth century?
    (a) the fishing industry
    (b) shipbuilding
    (c) the financial community
    (d) various domestic industries

_____3. The Mississippi Company:
    (a) had a monopoly on trade with France's Louisiana colony in America
    (b) managed the French national debt for five-year-old King Louis XV in a deal set by the king's gambling uncle
    (c) lost enormously in a stock fiasco called the "Mississippi Bubble"
    (d) all of these

_____4. During the eighteenth century the English Parliament was dominated by:
    (a) bankrupt but ambitious aristocrats
    (b) poor politicians with votes to sell
    (c) owners of property, especially the rich
    (d) representatives of the people

_____5. As one moved farther eastward in Europe in the eighteenth century there was increasing likelihood of finding:
    (a) rotten boroughs
    (b) serfdom
    (c) prominent intellectuals
    (d) larger navies.

_____6. During this period of time Sweden lost power, in part, through a military which:
    (a) invaded Russia and was lashed by the brutal winter
    (b) ran out of economic resources
    (c) lost its monopoly over the sea
    (d) all of these

_____ 7. In the eighteenth century, Russia won a port on the Baltic and gave the Swedes their major defeat in the battle of:
    (a) Poltava
    (b) Regensburg
    (c) Narva
    (d) none of these

_____8. The powerful political barrier whose crumbling allowed Russia and Hapsburg Austria to expand was:
(a) the Ottoman Empire
(b) Poland
(c) the Prussian Junker League
(d) Islam's sudden, permanent decline

_____9. The General-Ober-Finanz-Kriegs-und-Domänen-Direktorium is normally associated with the state of:
(a) Russia
(b) Poland
(c) Prussia
(d) the Holy Roman Empire

_____10. In the seventeenth century, the Netherlands:
(a) became the most urban region in Europe
(b) dominated Baltic trade through its shipping fleet
(c) boasted the most advanced financial system in Europe
(d) all of these

_____11. In the eighteenth century, the Dutch economy weakened through:
(a) a parasitic infection wiping out Baltic herring, the main catch of commercial fleets
(b) loss of its technological lead in shipbuilding
(c) urban riots let by witch-hunting gangs hostile to Dutch religious tolerance of Jews
(d) none of these

True/False

_____1. Dutch paintings of the eighteenth century combined scientific accuracy and displays of abundance—such as depicting exotic flowers—with sunny backdrops to protest Calvinist frugality.

_____2. A leading feature of French political life in the eighteenth century until the French Revolution (1789) was the attempt of the nobility to limit monarchical power.

_____3. Louis XV of France is considered a failure not only because of his mediocrity but because he was never properly trained as a ruler, was lazy, and was given to vice.

_____4. Both Whigs and Tories were proponents of the status quo in England, yet the Tories supported urban commercial interests and were in favor of religious toleration in general.

_____5. Robert Walpole's success resulted from his careful use of government patronage and manipulation of the House of Commons.

_____6. By the end of the seventeenth century, warfare and the resultant shifting political loyalties had become basic ingredients of life in central Europe.

_____7. The Pragmatic Sanction was designed to insure the succession to the Austrian throne of Maria Theresa.

_____8. Frederick II (Hohenzollern) of Prussia married Maria Theresa (Hapsburg) of Austria to insure his title to the lands of Prussia.

_____9. As a result of frequent revolutions, military conspiracies, and assassinations, the Romanovs only ruled Russia for 100 years.

_____10. By the middle of the eighteenth century, Russia was Europe's largest producer of iron.

Completion

1. The seven provinces that would become the United Netherlands first asserted their independence as a revolt together against _____ in 1592.

2. Though not having the power to legislate, the _____ of France became effective centers of resistance to royal authority.

3. The most influential minister in the reign of France's Louis XV was the aged _____ .

4. In reality _____ could be considered the first Prime Minister of Great Britain.

5. When soldiers of the Ottoman Empire laid siege to the city of _____ many of the people there welcomed the Turks as liberators from Roman Catholicism.

6. The *liberum veto* was a practice exercised in the central legislative assembly of _____ .

7. The rise of the Hohenzollern family to control Prussia began with their rule of the German territory of _____ .

8. _____ were the important class of German nobility influential throughout Prussian history.

9. In 1722 Peter the Great attempted to rearrange the Russian nobility through the _____ .

10. An early attempt at religious reform in Russia was led by the Patriarch _____ .

For Further Consideration

1. How did Britain's governing structures grow stronger in the eighteenth century, while corruption also thrived? Or was corruption part of the success? Use examples. You may also write as if you were an insider in Parliament, if you like.

2. Looking at the Ottoman Empire in the sixteenth and seventeenth centuries, what does the text say about the causes of its coming apart, producing "political and ethnic turmoil that still continues" to today? (See p. 281 and earlier, p. 231) What questions, of any, do you have about the Ottomans? Islam?

3. How does the development of central authority in Prussia differ from that in other European states during this period? How was it similar?

4. Describe several successes or partial successes of Peter the Great. If it helps, name a problem which Russia faced and then say what actions Peter took to change the situation. You may also write as if you were Peter himself.

5. What similarities do you see in the role of the early eighteenth-century nobles in Poland, Russia, Austria, Habsburg, and Sweden around their ruler's power? How did this compare with aristocrats in France? In England?

6. Imagine that you can have your pick of work in Amsterdam, the leading financial center of Europe in the mid-eighteenth century. Describe briefly the leading industries. Then say where you choose to work. You may also include going overseas to a colony, joining the military or the States General or a religious institution, or becoming an artist or other eighteenth-century occupation. Say briefly what you expect from your choice.

Answers

Multiple-Choice

		Text page
1.	C	274
2.	C	276
3.	D	276
4.	C	279
5.	B	280
6.	D	280, 287
7.	A	280, 287
8.	A	281
9.	C	284
10.	D	276-277
11.	B	275

True/False

1.	F	277
2.	T	276
3.	T	278
4.	F	278
5.	T	279
6.	T	280
7.	T	283
8.	F	283
9.	F	285
10.	T	286

Completion

1.	Spain	275
2.	*parlements*	276
3.	Cardinal Fleury	278
4.	Robert Walpole	279
5.	Vienna	281
6.	Poland	281
7.	Brandenburg	283
8.	Junkers	284
9.	Table of Ranks	286
10.	Nikon	286

16
Society and Economy Under the Old Regime in the Eighteenth Century

Commentary

The *old regime* is a generally descriptive term applied to life in Europe before the French Revolution. The term covers practically every facet of European social, economic, and political development before 1789.

Nowhere was the inherent harshness of the old regime experienced more than among the poorer classes. The poor worked the land or peopled the least savory areas of the urban landscape. Though conditions varied throughout Europe, peasants on the land or in the cities suffered at the hands of tyrannical landlords, oppressive styles of government, and a routinely harsh daily life. This situation did not suddenly improve with the development of the so-called "Agricultural Revolution." On the contrary, the initial advances brought on by the increased agricultural output favored the landlords and the middlemen instead of the persons working the land.

Family structures changed for working people. Formerly, the family worked as a unit, with everyone contributing to their home economy. But new machines in agriculture, in the manufacturing of textiles, and in heavy industry broke up the old home-economy. A factory-centered economy grew. For instance, where families and especially women had done handweaving and spinning at home, the invention of the spinning jenny in 1765 and the steam engine in 1769 mechanized the process. Men took the new jobs in factories, becoming dominant breadwinners. Women fell down the hierarchy, reduced to lower-skilled, lower-paying work, either in the factories, or in piecework at home, or in domestic service for richer families. So women's social and economic status fell as new technology moved industry forward.

Another pressure under eighteenth-century daily life came in an expanding population, especially in towns and cities. Europe's population—excluding the European provinces of the Ottoman Empire—nearly doubled between 1700 and 1800, growing to 190 million people. Although more than three quarters of all Europeans remained in the countryside, towns began to expand vigorously, partly from simple births and partly from migrations off the countryside—including from forced enclosures of common land. The results were dramatic. In 1500, Europe—excluding Hungary and Russia—had only 156 cities with populations over 10,000. By 1800 such cities had more than doubled, up to 363. Over the century, the number of cities of more than 100,000 people quadrupled from the big four—Paris, Milan, Venice, and Naples—to seventeen. Cities also grew from within. London, for instance, rose from 700,000 to a million residents.

Such growth in both rural and urban areas pushed demand for food, housing, and all necessities. A consumer market based on creating styles of beer or soap or foodstuffs began. Wedgwood china, a prestigious dinnerware up to today, was founded by Josiah Wedgwood as luxury china for royalty, with imitations for the growing middle class.

The growth in markets pressed for increased production, inspiring innovations in agriculture and manufacturing. This *Industrial Revolution* also drew in labor from the increased population and started a new-style, small-factory workforce, at first in rural areas and then in towns and cities. Such changes marked an early stage in what would evolve into modern industry over the next 200 years. Historians mark the starting time of the *Industrial Revolution* as the second half of the eighteenth century.

What else distinguished the *Industrial Revolution*? A series of technical innovations changed family life, work, towns and country, and the social fabric of Europe and the New World in fundamental ways. New scientific methods and tools, evolving from the "Scientific Revolution" (see Chapter 14) were applied to the production of food, textiles, iron, and other essentials, and the processes of production were transformed in astonishing ways. For instance, the steam engine provided a new source of energy over animals, wind, or water. Steam allowed factories to be moved from rural areas dependent on watermills into towns. The engine also allowed the pumping of dangerous water from mines. Inventions came in iron production in the form of the blast furnace, the rolling mill, and other techniques.

Furthermore, these inventions, plus population growth, plus the expanding classes of people under a small closed class of aristocrats stirred up social tensions. A diverse middle class growing richer from trade and commerce became increasingly restive for political influence and prestige. To win what they wanted, this class was willing to part with traditions. Such willingness would contribute to revolutions.

But for most of the century, despite the changes underway throughout society, the position of the aristocrats at the top of the *ancien regime* remained powerful. The eighteenth century was the age for aristocrats. They were small in number—in Great Britain, for example, only about 400 families—and generally represented fewer than 5 percent of any population. Yet they remained the wealthiest, most influential social class, with land ownership and control over tenant peasants and serfs as their economic base. The aristocracy maintained political rule by entering government personally, and they branched out into professions or the clergy.

Below the aristocrats, classes of urban dwellers were spreading. The bourgeoisie or middle class led the way, prospering from wealth independent of land. They would challenge the dominance of the nobility in different countries in the nineteenth century. This bourgeoisie was not a single homogenous unit, but it included conflicting and far-ranging sides: merchants, manufacturers, prosperous artisans and professional people and others should be in competition with each other. What they shared in common was a stake in the new economic order developing from innovations in agriculture, in commerce, in manufacturing, in trade and colonial expansion overseas, and in the growth of cities with their ports and markets and workforces. The middle class was the most dynamic of the all the classes of the *ancien regime*.

Further down the social ladder in town the lower classes also increased. They included an even more varied lot. A poor artisan class, for example, might include poor shopkeepers as well as artisans and wage-earners. All were an important part of the growing commercial urban life. At the hard bottom of towns and cities survived the poorest workers—employed or not. All the lower classes, however, were vulnerable, focusing on daily needs. Although poverty could be worse in the countryside, the spinoffs of poverty—crime, prostitution, begging, alcoholism—showed up more in the cities. Segregated districts, mainly in Eastern Europe, housed the Jewish communities or ghettos. Forbidden by Christian rulers to own land, most Jews were poor tradespeople and professionals. Christian peasants who left the land to live in town could face utter degradation. Public tortures and executions of criminals provided the spectacles for Europe's cities in this overall culture. This brutal scene of eighteenth-century urban poverty—in London, for example—was captured by artists like William Hogarth.

The mix of all these changes in social relations and economy foreshadowed city life as societies know today. The changes would also challenge the aristocracy and the ancien regime for political power before the century ended.

Identifications

Identify each one of the following as used in the text. Refer to the text as necessary.

	Text Page
ancien régime	289-290
hobereaux	291
taille	291
corveés	291
aristocratic resurgence	292
banalités	292
Ottoman Empire's peasants	292
Pugachev's Rebellion	293
servants	293-294
genre painting	296
infanticide	298
crop rotation	299
potato	300-304
Industrial Revolution	200
Josiah Wedgwood	301
domestic system (a.k.a. *putting out*)	302
James Hargreaves	302
James Watt	302
bourgeoisie	305
"just price"	306
"riff-raff"	306
"court Jews"	307

Map Exercise A

Outline/locate each of the following on the accompanying map:

Countries	Capital Cities	Water Bodies/Rivers
1. England	9. London	17. Thames
2. Scotland	10. Edinburgh	18. Firth of Forth
3. Ireland	11. Dublin	19. Irish Sea
4. France	12. Paris	20. Seine
5. Prussia	13. Berlin	21. Oder
6. Poland	14. Warsaw	22. Vistula
7. Austria	15. Vienna	23. Danube
8. Russia	16. Saint Petersburg	24. Gulf of Finland

Do your own research, using maps from throughout the text and also see page vi of this guide for additional references.

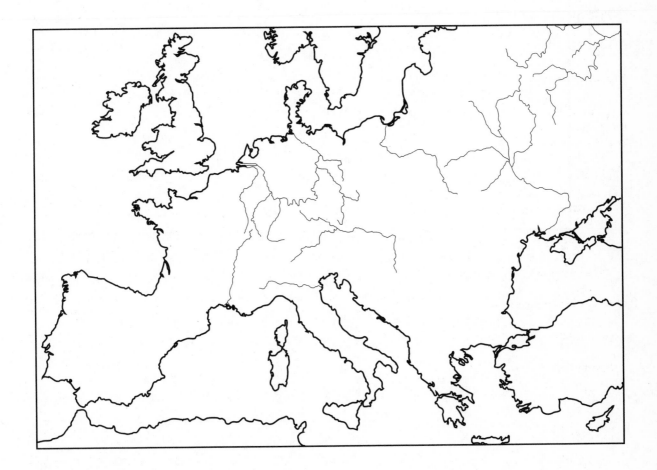

Graph Exercise B

Referring to the statistics presented on p. 300 of the text, prepare a graph (or spreadsheet) demonstrating the growth of European population from 1700 to 1850 or the closest year cited. To enhance your understanding of the demographics of this era, research similar statistics for the thirteen British colonies in North America that became the United States during this same period.

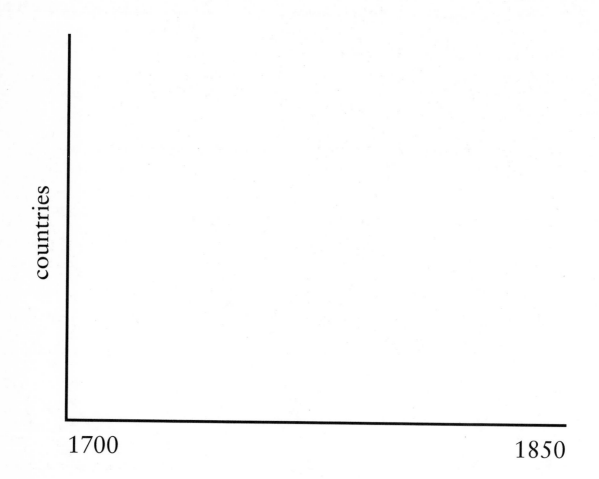

Short-Answer Exercises

Multiple-Choice

_____1. According to the textbook the old regime was characterized by all of the following except:
(a) absolute monarchy
(b) an agrarian economy
(c) aristocratic elites
(d) Protestant domination

_____2. Britain's ruling aristocratic families in the eighteenth century numbered only:
(a) 20
(b) 400
(c) 100
(d) 800

_____3. In which of the following places did the nobility reckon their wealth in "souls"?
(a) Russia
(b) Poland
(c) Austria
(d) The Papal States

_____4. Population growth during the eighteenth century appears to be caused mainly by all of the following except:
(a) fewer wars and epidemics
(b) superior advances in medical knowledge and techniques
(c) a decline in the death rate
(d) changes in the supply and quality of food

_____5. During this century which of the following was not a contributing factor to Britain's industrial development?
(a) generally low taxes
(b) highly stratified class structure
(c) rich deposits of coal and iron
(d) few internal trade barriers

_____6. Which of the following developed techniques that moved cotton production from the home to the factory?
(a) Richard Arkwright
(b) Henry Cort
(c) Edmund Cartwright
(d) James Hargreaves

_____7. The machine most responsible for bringing about the combination of industrialization with urbanization was the:
(a) power loom
(b) flying shuttle
(c) steam engine
(d) spinning jenny

_____8. Surprisingly, in this era poverty was:
    (a) worse in the cities
    (b) rarely punished
    (c) almost nonexistent
    (d) worse in the countryside

_____9. Which of the following statements is most correct about the emerging middle class in Europe?
    (a) the land was not a primary source of middle class income
    (b) they feared the lower classes
    (c) they lived chiefly in the towns and cities
    (d) all of these are correct statements about the middle class of this era

_____10. What is not true about eighteenth-century society?
    (a) Cities were commonly run by self-perpetrating oligarchies of nobles and the richest commercial families.
    (b) The lower classes of shopkeepers, artisans, and wage earners were the largest urban group.
    (c) All classes resisted shopping, until industrially produced bread became cheaper than home-baked.
    (d) The Industrial Revolution created a new kind of workforce.

_____11. Becoming a mother in the eighteenth century often meant:
    (a) risking dangerous disease to give birth.
    (b) having a child in poverty.
    (c) giving the baby to a wet nurse and going back to work to support the family economy.
    (d) all of the above

_____12. Unless she were rich, a married woman in the eighteenth century:
    (a) devoted herself to do her housekeeping or childrearing.
    (b) earned household money working in the industrialized textile factories.
    (c) often worked as a servant.
    (d) primarily worked under her husband's authority in the farm or family trade.

True/False

_____1. Oddly, in their desire to maintain traditional rights, both 18th-century peasants and aristocrats sought to protect existing privileges.

_____2. At this time approximately 95–99% of the populations of the various European countries would be considered non-aristocratic.

_____3. The practice of young men and women moving away from home was known as neocolonialism.

_____4. In non-aristocratic households the males were expected to do virtually all the work of the family unit.

_____5. The eighteenth century saw a stabilization of the numbers of children admitted to foundling homes.

_____6. Though upsetting the political structure, industrialization permitted greater control over the forces of nature than had ever been possible before.

_____7. Edmund Cartwright developed the power loom in the 1780s.

_____8. Generally, the emerging middle class feared those below them and resented those above them in society.

_____9. A change in clothing prices is generally considered the most common spark to urban riots in this era.

_____10. As we know it today, the desire to make money and accumulate profits, the so-called "commercial spirit," really gained freer play in the eighteenth century.

Completion

1. Eighteenth-century French aristocracy was basically divided into the nobility of the _____ and the nobility of the _____ .

2. Though enjoying many privileges the French nobility were liable for a tax known as the _____ .

3. _____ constituted the economic basis of eighteenth-century life.

4. The great peasant uprising in Russia during the reign of Catherine the Great was led by _____ .

5. The first practical steam engine was invented by _____ .

6. The new puddling process, which vastly improved the qualities of the iron produced, was developed by _____ .

7. During the eighteenth century, Europe's most populous city was _____ .

8. The engravings of _____ portray the problems caused by urbanization in London during the mid-eighteenth century.

9. Urban _____ during this era were generally well-organized actions against price increases in food.

10. Throughout the era of the old regime European _____ were considered socially and religiously inferior.

For Further Consideration

1. Imagine that you live in an eighteenth-century, non-aristocratic family of your choice. Briefly describe your family economy. For instance, what does the family do for work? Farming? Shopkeeping? Are you miners? or craftsmen or merchants or wage-earners? In what town or village? What role do you play? How does your family operate to bring in food and other necessities? What reminds you of families that you know today?

2. Take sides over the enclosure of the common land in your English village. Imagine that you are a poor farmer talking with friends over potato soup in your kitchen. What are at least two fears or other effects you discuss about the enclosure? What did you hear that the rich landlord likes about the enclosures? Write at least three things.

3. Technical inventions pushed forward Britain's early industrial revolution. Select at least two new machines or processes and describe how they worked. What effect did they have on production? On workers (when you know)? Inventions may be in agriculture, manufacturing, or heavy industry.

Alternative essay: Write about only one machine or process and any connection you see between this machine and the discoveries of the scientific revolution (i.e. astronomy, physics, scientific method, etc.). Or look back a bit further and write what you see of connections between the printing press and paper with the industrial revolution.

4. Why was the comparatively small middle class considered the most dynamic of the eighteenth-century urban classes?

5. What do you see that rural riots by peasants and urban riots had in common, if anything? Causes? Participants? Other characteristics? How did they differ? What, if anything, reminds you of riots today?

Answers

Multiple-Choice

			Text page
1.	D		289-290
2.	B		290
3.	A		293
4.	B		300
5.	A		301
6.	A		302
7.	C		302
8.	D		305
9.	D		305
10.	C		300
11.	D		295, 297
12.	D		298

True/False

1.	T	293
2.	T	290
3.	F	294
4.	F	295
5.	F	298
6.	T	300
7.	T	302
8.	T	305
9.	F	306
10.	T	308

Completion

1.	sword/robe	291
2.	vingtieme/twentieth	291
3.	land	292
4.	Emelyan Pugachev	293
5.	Thomas Newcomen	302-303
6.	Henry Cort	303
7.	London	304
8.	William Hogarth	305
9.	riots	306
10.	Jews	307

17

Empire, War, and Colonial Rebellion

Commentary

By the eighteenth century, armies no longer fought under exclusively religious banners. Wars began openly over competition among European states for control of land and people and other resources to trade in the continent, in the New World, and elsewhere. Because Europeans enjoyed wealth and superior technology in the sixteenth and seventeenth centuries, they could conquer overseas areas and begin empires. In the eighteenth century Europeans expanded these empires. From the perspective of European colonists, pirates, traders, soldiers, and monarchs, the world was there for the taking.

A key feature of the empire's settlements in North America was slavery. Slavery grew out of a severe labor shortage in the New World. Europeans enslaved Africans to work after the Ottoman Empire prohibited the exportation of white slaves from its territory and after native Americans began dying out from disease, forced labor, and wars of resistance. The importation and exploitation of Africans began in 1619 in Jamestown, Virginia. The trade mushroomed into a major transatlantic commercial operation bringing in millions of slaves over three centuries. Considerable profits were made in a complex new economy based on slave labor. This economic network profited local colonial planters and mine owners, slave traders, European and American manufacturers, African tribal leaders, bankers, and many others. Slavery was both brutal and productive so long as fresh supplies of slaves could be gotten. At the same time, the Africans made profound contributions to the new cultures that rooted themselves in the Western Hemisphere. Africans not only built many of America's plantations but also contributed innovations to music, food, furniture, and other aspects of life in the settlements. At the same time, the scale of the slave trade and the creation of societies so dependent on slave labor was new in world history. Every nation today where slavery operated still struggles with the legacy of racism and other effects.

The culture which slavery supported also produced a theory of empire called mercantilism. Mercantilists believed that bullion determined a country's wealth and so policies should be promoted to increase the accumulation of such gold and silver. Mercantilists also assumed the world's resources were limited so that one nation's economy had to grow at the expense of others. The well-being of the home country lived at the cost of the colony.

Mercantilism could not be forced to work, though. Colonial and home markets did not mesh. For instance, Spain could not manufacture enough goods for all of South America. Spain, France, and England, by diverse means, attempted to maintain a favorable balance of or even monopoly of trade with their colonies. But the French and British colonists competed with each other over control of the rich plantations in the West Indies and over India as well. Mercantile rivalries led to wars, drawing in allies. The battles culminated in great wars at mid-century where England and France fought over colonial power in North America and also sought to take advantage of Spanish weaknesses in holding her Latin American possessions, and Prussia challenged Austria's influence in central Europe.

When the wars ended with the treaties of Hubertusberg and Paris in 1763, Spain was forced to take defeat and infiltration by the British. Prussia became a major power, reducing the Austria-Hapsburg Empire to a shell—mainly Hungary. France ceased to be a great colonial power while Great Britain's empire expanded by taking over the French slave trade in the New World and French-held areas of India. Indeed, never before had a European power experienced such military success on a global scale as did Great Britain.

In the New World, however, Great Britain's winning supremacy also planted the seeds of the revolution for American independence. The vast territories held by France were handed over to England with the peace. Yet, French-British rivalry continued into the American War for Independence. The trail of immediate events leading to the independence struggle began over the cost of Great Britain's just-previous war against France. Great Britain went to the colonies, seeking taxes to pay for war and administration of the colonies. The Americans would not accept Parliament's determination of what was necessary. Now distant from their home country, the American, were self-assured and began expressing a vision of their own future free of London's influences. By employing arguments that had influenced British political thought over the previous one hundred years, and by steadfastly refusing to submit to British authority, they soon drew the issue between "mother" and "daughter" states. By the spring of 1775 the colonies had organized and begun to marshal public opinion against George III's government. In the accompanying pamphleteering, Thomas Paine's *Common Sense* enlarged the view that separation was the answer. After eight years of intermittent fighting, a second Peace of Paris (1783) recognized the independence of Britain's former seaboard colonies as the United States of America. Having declared their independence in 1776 these areas were free to experiment with political, social, and economic activities unheard of in previous centuries. One of the most innovative was the concept of government by popular consent rather than by the king, divine, or natural law, or some other tradition. Although women, slaves, and Native Americans were left out of government, the American Revolution opened the way for further experiments towards the ideal of democracy. These experiments, some successful, reflected the thinking of the time, the Enlightenment, and also the unique character of American frontier life. The ideas they embodied have become part of the Western heritage.

Identifications

Identify each one of the following as used in the text. Refer to the text as necessary.

	Text page
mercantilism	312
Casa de Contratación	313
slave ship *Brookes*	316
Treaty of Utrecht	319
asiento	319
Convention of Westminster	320
Prince Kaunitz	320
Treaty of Hubertusberg	320
Watson and the Shark by John Copley	318
Pitt the Elder	320-321
Battle of Plassey	321
Treaty of Paris (1763)	321
Charles Townshend	322
Lord North & the "Intolerable Acts"	322
Quebec Act	322
Treaty of Paris (1783)	323
Common Sense by Thomas Paine	323
The Commonwealthmen	323
John Wilkes	324
Christopher Wyvil	324
Pitt the Younger	325

Map Exercise A

Locate each of the following on the accompanying map:

1. Colonial Empire of Great Britain before 1763
2. Colonial Empire of France before 1763
3. Colonial Empire of Spain
4. Dutch colonies in the New World
5. The West Indies

Do your own research, using maps from throughout the text and also see page vi of this guide for additional references.

Map Exercise B

On this map of the eastern seaboard of North America, mark each of the thirteen British colonies founded there after 1607. Mark the largest or major city (town) in each in the year 1776.

Do your own research, using maps from throughout the text and also see page vi of this guide for additional references.

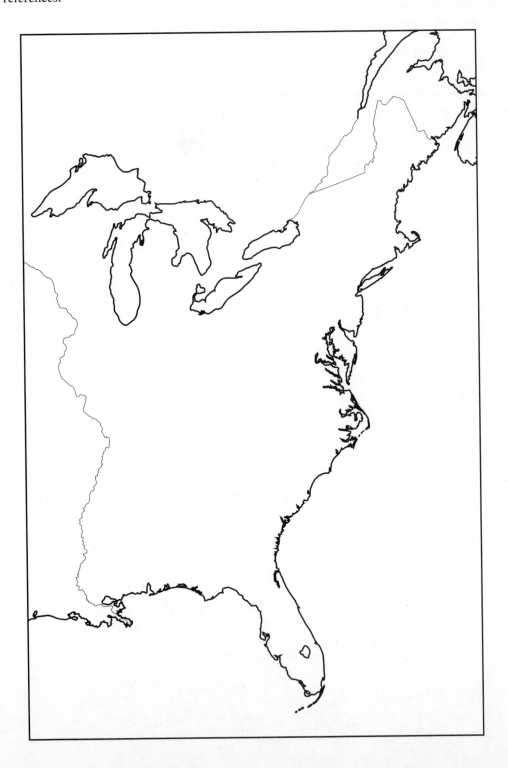

Short-Answer Exercises

Multiple-Choice

_____1. European contacts with the rest of the world have passed through how many distinct stages?
(a) 3
(b) 4
(c) 5
(d) 6

_____2. The European domination of the world was based on:
(a) location
(b) cultural superiority
(c) technological advances
(d) none of these were factors

_____3. The most influential part of Spain's efforts to regulate trade with her possessions in the New World was the:
(a) viceroys
(b) *flota* system
(c) *Casa de Contratación*
(d) Peninsulares

_____4. Competition in eighteenth-century trade included everything but:
(a) smuggling and piracy
(b) reliance on naval protection
(c) slave labor
(d) independent colonial markets

_____5. Empress Maria Theresa's arrangement with the _____ preserved the state in the eighteenth century but actually hampered later development.
(a) Prussians
(b) Turks
(c) Poles
(d) Magyars

_____6. Which of the following treaties ended the war in which French aid to Prussia helped consolidate a new, powerful German state?
(a) Treaty of Paris
(b) Treaty of Aix-la-Chapelle
(c) Treaty of Westphalia
(d) Treaty of Utrecht

_____7. The root cause of the American colonial revolt against Great Britain was concern over:
(a) imperial taxation
(b) imperial policy toward the western lands
(c) imperial control of colonial finances
(d) all of these

_____8. Initially, the Second Continental Congress was:
        (a) belligerent
        (b) promonarchy
        (c) conciliatory
        (d) none of these.

_____9. Which of the following documents had the most effect on the American struggle for
        independence?
        (a) *The Treaty of Paris*
        (b) *Convention of Westminster*
        (c) *Common Sense*
        (d) *Cato's Letters*

_____10. Which of the following is most correct about the American Revolution?
        (a) Slaves were freed.
        (b) It was truly a radical revolution.
        (c) Its ideas were limited to North America.
        (d) It encouraged socialism.

_____11. Europeans went to Africa in continuous trade to get slaves because:
        (a) white slaves were not available from the Ottoman Empire.
        (b) it was cheaper to import new slaves to the New World than create living conditions on
            plantations that let slaves survive.
        (c) the native Americans were an inadequate source, dying in hard labor, disease, and wars
            of resistance.
        (d) all of the above

_____12. Plantation slaves in North America:
        (a) preserved some aspects of their ancestral religions, one of which was Islam.
        (b) practiced no religion other than an innocent jungle faith in eating, sleeping, and sexual
            play.
        (c) readily became Christians once they married in their master's church.

True/False

_____1. Armies to protect colonial, religious settlers were the most important feature of eighteenth-
        century mercantile empires.

_____2. Joseph Dupleix and Robert Clive are both important names associated with the European
        colonization efforts in India.

_____3. For Spain the governmental structure in the colonies was designed to augment commercial
        goals.

_____4.   Generally speaking, most laws governing slavery were designed to protect those held in
        bondage from the excessive cruelties of their masters.

_____5. In reality, the British right secured in the Treaty of Utrecht to send one ship per year to the
        great trading fair at Portobello, Panama, opened the door to vast smuggling opportunities.

_____6. The real surprise in the so-called "diplomatic revolution" of 1756 was the British-French settlement of outstanding colonial differences.

_____7. Throughout his career Count Anton Kaunitz, the Austrian foreign minister, was determined to maintain a German-based alliance with Prussia.

_____8. The 1773 Tea Act that triggered the Boston Tea Party actually had lowered the price of tea for the colonies.

_____9. The government's right of taxation, the arbitrary power of the monarchy, and the perceived corruption of the House of Commons were all factors influencing American opinion on the eve of the War of Independence.

_____10. The American revolutionaries not only aimed to win colonial independence but to create a new kind of government based on popular consent.

_____11. During the first four centuries of settlement in the New World–up to the twentieth century–far more black slaves arrived involuntarily than Europeans who chose to come.

Completion

1. Virtually all the colonial powers had possessions in the islands of the _____ Sea.

2. The governing principle behind all colonization in this era was the theory of _____.

3. A shortage of _____ was a driving force in the slave trade.

4. A conflict starting over a body part and involving Great Britain's rivalry with Spain during this period was a 1739 conflict known as the War of _____ .

5. Britain's victories in Europe and North America were engineered by Secretary of State _____ .

6. The British ministry under George Grenville passed the _____ Act which was symbolic of Britain's need for additional revenue.

7. The _____ crisis set the stage for years of struggle between Britain and her American colonies, finally leading to the latter's independence.

8. Political theory that inspired the successful American drive for independence can be found in the 17th century struggle in England against the _____ .

9. _____ was the English monarch throughout the period of the American revolution.

10. Internal opposition to the king of Great Britain can be associated with the group known as the _____ .

For Further Consideration

1. Describe briefly the four stages in Europe's development of empires overseas. What was one or two harmful effects which empires created? What do you see as one or two contributions of the empire to human progress?

2. Imagine that your are an eighteenth-century Spaniard (or European of your choice) who owns a gold mine in South America. You've been asked to define mercantilism and how gold fits into mercantilism by the colonial newspaper. Write a short paragraph.

3. Looking at slavery, list at least three ways in which slavery profited either a slave trader or a plantation owner. Then list at least four ways in which slavery hurt the slaves. Describe one way that language sometimes helped the slaves organize and revolt.

4. If you were a rebellious North American in the 1750s and 1760s, angry at the British, what are several grievances that drove you to revolution? You may write them in a list or a paragraph, or as banner slogans for a public protest.

5. Can you relate the Association Movement in England to the American Revolution? Use specific examples as necessary to support your answer.

Answers

Multiple-Choice

		Text page
1.	B	311
2.	C	311
3.	C	313
4.	D	312
5.	D	320
6.	B	320
7.	D	321-323
8.	C	323
9.	C	323
10.	B	325
11.	D	315-316
12.	A	317

True/False

1.	F	312
2.	T	312
3.	T	313
4.	F	317
5.	T	319
6.	F	320
7.	F	320
8.	T	322
9.	T	321-324
10.	T	325
11.	T	316

Completion

1.	Caribbean	312
2.	mercantilism	312
3.	labor	315
4.	Jenkins' Ear	319
5.	William Pitt, the Elder	320-321
6.	Sugar	321
7.	Stamp Act	322
8.	Stuarts	323
9.	George III	323
10.	Whigs	323-324

18
The Age of Enlightenment: Eighteenth-Century Thought

Commentary

The Enlightenment is the broad term applied to the intellectual developments of the eighteenth century. These developments were sponsored by a relatively small number of thinkers and writers primarily throughout western Europe. Their work and thoughts set the stage for much of our thinking today. What these philosophers advocated were related ideas in two areas: personal freedoms and the reform of existing conditions and institutions. By so doing they provided an important part of the background for the many social, political, and economic changes that occurred in this era.

Although the seeds for much of the Enlightenment's emphasis can be found in the moderate political and social atmosphere of England, France was the heart of the movement. French writers such as Voltaire and Montesquieu were pioneers in championing Enlightenment ideas. By the middle of the eighteenth century reformers were sharpening their criticism and pointing increasingly to specific problems within the *ancien régime*.

With a new definition of the role of nature in human life the *philosophes* proposed changes in most aspects of existence. The increased knowledge at their disposal, as exemplified by the *Encyclopedia,* made them confident that their reforms were both reasonable and possible. Increased knowledge and rationality, the reformers hoped, would be the keys to both the immediate and the long-range effects of their work.

In a number of areas one can trace the thoughts of the eighteenth-century intellectuals: The concept of deism, for example, provided a means by which thinkers could accept the new rationalism without specifically denying the role of the supernatural (God) in human life. The organized religions, however, especially the Catholic Church, were being held up to considerable ridicule stemming from the *philosophes'* view of the medieval nature of religion. The rationalists of the eighteenth century were not prepared to accept what they believed to be the oppressive and irrational views of the Roman Church. The *philosophes* also often attacked Judaism. Some viewed Judaism as a more primitive faith than Christianity. Two Jewish intellectuals countered with rational arguments. Baruch Spinoza wrote that all religions should be subject to rational analysis, and he closely identified God with nature. He was charged by Jews and Christians with atheism and excommunicated from his synagogue. Some *philosophes* then saw him as a martyr and softened, advocating opening society for fuller participation by Jews. After Spinoza, Moses Mendelssohn took a less-extreme tack. He argued there were many paths to God with Judaism as one. He emphasized that ethical behavior was the common goal and that different faiths should not only tolerate each other but also allow for wide differences within. At the same time the *philosophes* called for and supported a greater degree of religious toleration for all the faiths of Europe.

The effect of the Enlightenment on society was to be profound. Its thinkers insisted that, like nature itself, society must be founded on a rational base. Where it was not, then changes, reforms, must be instituted. The humane considerations of Cesare Beccaria and Jeremy Bentham should be noted in this regard. The attention given to economic systems by prominent Enlightenment thinkers should also be observed. Adam Smith's position raised many new questions about the existing mercantile practices of the time and remained the philosophical basis for much of this period of industrialization. His work, *The Wealth of Nations,* has remained fundamental to Western society's debate over economic progress and individual well-being.

It is in the area of political thought that the *philosophes* have continued to have the greatest impact right to the present day. Not since the ancient Greeks had the foundations of the systems by which human beings have governed themselves been opened to so much investigation and criticism. The *philosophes,* in sometimes widely varying approaches, were attempting to find the rationality behind Europe's governmental systems and in so doing they became involved in discussions and advocated changes that cut across the social and political base of existing institutions. Going well beyond mere criticism of corruption in government and church, the *philosophes* sought to establish a new set of fundamentals by which human beings could reasonably be governed in the future. For example, Montesquieu outlined a system of government calling for a division of political authority into three distinct branches of government. To take another example, Rousseau approached politics from a moral view, raising questions such as, "Was the purpose of life to mainly consume and make commerce and industry?" Rousseau said a moral human being was the goal, and that producing one was the real work of society. Indeed, society, wrote Rousseau, was more important than its individual members in that society shaped its views on women. Rousseau wrote that women should be excluded from public affairs and confined to the home, with duties centered around bearing and raising children and pleasing men. Such sexism in the *philosophes* produced a defense of women's rights by Mary Wollstonecraft. Wollstonecraft argued that confining women to the home amounted to sexual slavery and male tyranny, and that human progress as a whole suffered when women were denied good educations. Thus she broadened the reform agenda of Enlightenment to include women's rights.

Rulers in eastern Europe adapted some of these Enlightenment ideas to govern in a style called *Enlightened Absolutism.* Kings and queens utilized select Enlightenment principles to strengthen their grip over their thrones and to also build up their military. Frederick II (the Great) of Prussia, Maria Theresa and her son Joseph II of Austria, and Catherine the Great of Russia variously pursued social and economic reforms espoused by the *philosophes.* Frederick of Prussia, for example, authorized more religious tolerance. But at the same time as Frederick established equal protection under the law for Catholics and Jews, he also had additional laws recodified. These cut the power of the aristocracy and extended the power of the throne. Similarly acting for self-interest, the rulers of the Austrian and Russian empires reversed themselves on reforms when the nobility and peasants took more liberty than the rulers planned. For instance, in Russia the Pugachev peasant revolt in 1771–1775 so frightened Catherine the Great that when the French Revolution broke out in 1789, she censored Enlightenment books and sent writers to Siberia. By the 1770s, however, Enlightenment thought had inspired another revolution in the English colonies of America. The outlook of the *philosophes* that championed the idea of change could not be exiled, but instead would change the world for centuries to come.

Identifications

Identify each one of the following as used in the text. Refer to the text as necessary.

	Text page
Newtonian world view	333
tabula rasa of John Locke	333
Candide	335
Denis Diderot	336
Baruch Spinoza	338
Cesare Beccaria	338
physiocrats	338-339
The Wealth of Nations	339
laissez-faire economics	339
The Persian Letters	340
The Spirit of the Laws	340-341
The Social Contract	341
Madame de Pompadour	341
Mary Wollstonecraft	342
Josephinism	344
robot	345
Peter III of Russia	345-346
Treaty of Kuchuk-Kainardji	346
partitions of Poland	346-347
Pugachev's Rebellion	348

Map Exercise A

Draw the boundaries of 18th-century Prussia, Austria, Hungary and Russia in relationship to the changing boundaries of Poland. Circle cities/centers of Enlightenment thought throughout Europe.

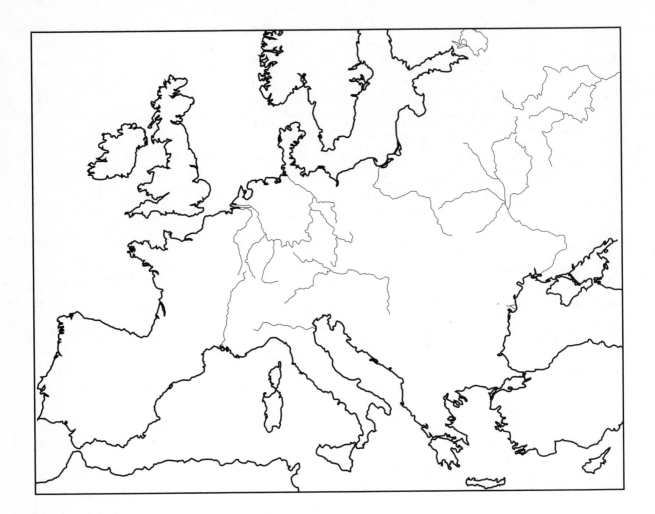

Map Exercise B

Mark the current boundaries of Germany, Poland, the Czech Republic, Slovakia, Hungary, Bulgaria, Rumania, Belorussia, Ukraine and Russia. Compare with Exercise A.

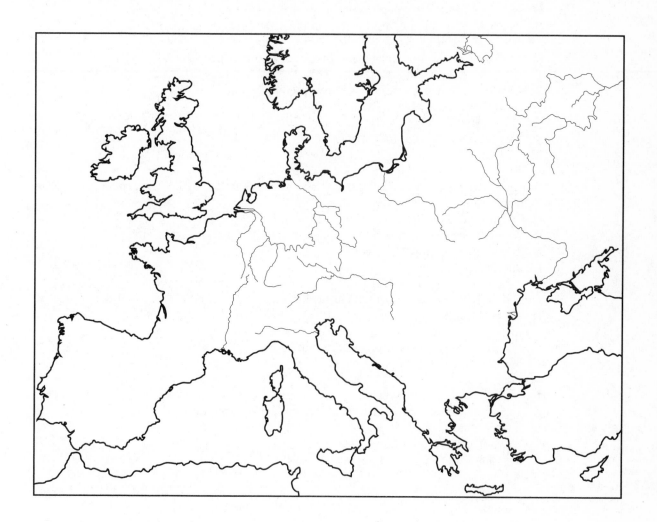

Short-Answer Exercises

Multiple-Choice

_____1. Which of the following is the least accurate statement about the *philosophes*?
(a) they were most often men from the upper classes of society
(b) they held a common desire for reform of society, government, and thought
(c) they used the printed word as their major weapon
(d) they were not well-organized and disagreed on many points

_____2. Which of the following works was not written by Voltaire?
(a) *Letters on the English*
(b) *The Persian Letters*
(c) *Elements of the Philosophy of Newton*
(d) *Candide*

_____3. Which is the most accurate statement about the churches of France during the Age of Enlightenment?
(a) they provided justification for the status quo
(b) the upper classes dominated the upper clergy
(c) they owned a great deal of land
(d) all of these.

_____4. During this period, Cesare Becarria argued, typically of the *philosophes,* that the purpose of laws was to achieve:
(a) justice for all classes
(b) the greatest good for the greatest number
(c) religious toleration for all peoples
(d) none of these.

_____5. Adam Smith's philosophy of economics basically advocated all but:
(a) increased tariff regulation
(b) free pursuit of economic self-interest
(c) exploitation of the earth's physical resources
(d) free trade

_____6. Montesquieu explored ideas for political reform because:
(a) he liked sociology, a popular new science
(b) peasant revolts threatened his estates
(c) he wanted to defend the French aristocracy from an oppressive, inefficient monarchy
(d) the British cabinet system impressed him as superior to the French

_____7. Which of the following was not written by Rousseau?
(a) *Nathan the Wise*
(b) *The Social Contract*
(c) *Discourse on the Moral Effects of the Arts and Sciences*
(d) *Discourse on the Origin of Inequality*

_____8. Reforming society to support the moral development of individual members is an idea associated with:
(a) Rousseau
(b) Madame de Pompadour and the court of Louis XV
(c) Bentham
(d) Catherine the Great of Russia

_____9. In the last analysis the Enlightened Monarchs of the eighteenth century supported change and innovation because:
   (a) of potential benefits leading to their military strength
   (b) it reduced their dependency on military strength
   (c) of a desire to impress their female subjects
   (d) all of these

_____10. Which of the following rulers is not normally associated with the ideas of Enlightened Absolutism?
   (a) Joseph II of Austria
   (b) Catherine the Great of Russia
   (c) George III of England
   (d) Frederick II of Prussia

_____11. Baruch Spinoza of the Netherlands contributed to the Enlightenment:
   (a) controversial ideas of God being closer to nature than to Scripture
   (b) advocacy of Judaism as a superior, rational faith
   (c) spiritual passion divorced from any thought of God
   (d) all of the above

True/False

_____1. A long-term effect of the Enlightenment has been the idea that change brings improvement within Western societies.

_____2. John Locke fully accepted the Christian view of humankind flawed by sin.

_____3. English societies of Freemasons were early advocates of reading and debate.

_____4. The Scottish *philosophe* David Hume's work challenging the idea of miracles was titled *Miracles of Miracles*.

_____5. Gotthold Lessing's *Nathan the Wise* actually called for the religious toleration of non-Christians.

_____6. François Quesnay headed a French mercantile association opposed to physiocratic thought.

_____7. Montesquieu's analysis of the separation of powers within the British constitutional system called attention to the role of patronage and corruption.

_____8. Rousseau's influence in Western thought ended with his death in 1778.

_____9. Mary Wollstonecraft argued that it was in a woman's best interest to be the sensual slave of man, especially her husband.

_____10. Leopold II, upon succession to the Austrian throne, repealed many of the reforms of his brother Joseph II.

_____11. Moses Mendelssohn, a leading Jewish intellectual, urged governments to maintain neutrality on religious issues in his book, *Jerusalem*.

Completion

1. In comparison to all others, _____ was the country with the greatest freedom of speech and press in the eighteenth century.

2. _____ was the English journal which encouraged a wider discussion of eighteenth-century ideas.

3. The publication of the _____ can be considered the greatest literary monument of the Enlightenment era.

4. The idea that was advanced in an attempt to establish a natural and rational base to religion was known as _____ .

5. *The Decline and Fall of the Roman Empire* was written by _____ .

6. The comment, "first servant of the State," is associated with _____ .

7. The most coldly rational of the so-called Enlightened Absolutists was _____ .

8. Catherine the Great of Russia was of _____ descent.

9. _____ was the title of a set of guidelines issued by Catherine the Great that reflected some of the political ideas of the Enlightenment.

10. During the second half of the eighteenth century the formal boundaries of _____ were removed from the map of Europe.

For Further Consideration

1. Explain the concept of deism. How is deism a reflection of Enlightenment thought?

2. Discuss the thinking and work of Baron Montesquieu. In your opinion what has been the long-term impact of his work?

3. Discuss the thinking and works of Jean Jacques Rousseau. In your opinion what has been the long-term impact of his work?

4. What is meant by the term Enlightened Absolutism? Select a monarch of the eighteenth century and give an example of how he/she applied Enlightened Absolutism.

5. Generally, how would you describe the overall impact of Enlightenment ideas on Europe? Consider these ideas as reflected in our own society today.

6. Optional: Name a *philosophe* of your choice and write one question you would ask this thinker about something not covered in the text so far (such as about slavery, Islam, etc.).

Answers

Multiple-Choice

		Text page
1.	A	332-333
2.	B	335-336
3.	D	336
4.	B	334
5.	A	339
6.	C	340
7.	A	340-341
8.	A	340-341
9.	A	342
10.	C	342, 347
11.	A	338

True/False

1.	T	331
2.	F	333
3.	T	335
4.	F	337
5.	T	337
6.	F	339
7.	F	340
8.	F	341
9.	F	342
10.	T	345
11.	T	338

Completion

1.	England	333
2.	*The Spectator*	335
3.	*Encyclopedia*	336
4.	deism	336-337
5.	Edward Gibbon	337
6.	Frederick the Great	342-343
7.	Joseph II of Austria	343
8.	German	345
9.	Instructions	346
10.	Poland	347

19
The French Revolution

Commentary

The French Revolution marked the political turning point to modern European history. It toppled the rule of the absolute monarchy and of the feudal aristocrats. In the process, the revolution also unleashed the poorest urban classes against the aristocracy, created Europe's first citizen army, tested Enlightenment ideas in politics, raised the middle classes into governing power, changed how social status was determined, and generally transformed the culture and economics of the society.

The chapter surveys the leading moments in the fast-changing, complex drama, beginning with a summary of French problems on the eve of the revolution. Conflicts escalate into the revolution of 1789, then backstep into a constitutional monarchy, then move on to the second revolution in 1792 and into the foreign wars which France also started that year. Finally comes the Reign of Terror in 1793 and its backlash the *Thermidor* in 1794.

What opened the way to revolution was a financial crisis in the government in the 1780s. Indeed, the monarchy found itself deep in debt while the aristocracy and new middle classes prospered. The government's crisis came from events reaching back half a century. Costing France were her wars, notable the Seven Years' War against England, and French support of the related colonial American Revolution. In the meantime, at the bottom of the economy, poor people went hungry and cold from meager harvests, food shortages, rising prices, wages not keeping pace, and an unusually cold winter in 1788. Seeking relief for itself, the monarchy tried to levy new taxes. The *parlements* of the aristocracy and the clergy resisted, declaring such taxes illegal and seeking public support for themselves as protectors of French liberty. Continuing conflict between Louis XVI and the aristocracy led to the convening of the Estates-General to decide the taxes. Since aristocrats and clergy had always dominated the Estates-General, the kings had not called a meeting since 1614. However, pressed against a wall of state debt, Louis XVI submitted to the convocation for May 5, 1789.

The meeting unleashed social and political forces that neither the nobles nor the king could control. The forces moved so swiftly that the calendar of changes in the revolution is counted by months rather than years. The Estates-General provided the stage for the opening moment with its three groups: the First Estate of the clergy, the Second Estate of the nobility, and the Third Estate of merchants, professionals, artisans, shopkeepers, workers, and peasants—that is, everyone else. At first, preparatory to the meeting, there came a political standoff over voting power among the estates in September 1788. Then, as the meeting finally convened in May 1789, the group presented a list of grievances *(cahiers de doleances)* to the king. After a month of stops and starts over procedural issues, in June leaders of the Third Estate took matters into their own hands. They invited the clergy and nobles to join the Third Estate in dissolving the Estates-General altogether and in setting up a new, legislative body, the National Constituent Assembly, which would then create a constitutional monarchy. While the king resisted, a month later, in July, bread riots broke out in Paris. On July 14, a poplar uprising spread after crowds stormed the Bastille fortress, seeking weapons and forming a citizens' militia. Mobs in provincial cities soon followed on to street riots, and rumors that the king's troops were coming to repress peasants swept a "Great Fear" through the countryside. Peasants burned chateaux and took scarce food and repossessed land they had lost in the "aristocratic resurgence" of the prior quarter century.

On the night of August 4, the aristocracy acted to head off loss of all their power by offering to give up some. They renounced feudal dues, rights and tithes and declared that all Frenchmen were now subject to the same laws. On August 27, the Assembly adopted the Declaration of the Rights of Man and Citizen.

The Declaration was a statement of principles to guide the writing of a new constitution. It affirmed that all men—not women—were equal and the inalienable rights, including liberty, personal safety, and property. It indicted the abuses of the absolute monarchy. It was the death certificate of the *ancien regime*. Louis XVI delayed giving his royal approval to the Declaration. A month later, on October 5, a crowd of thousands of Parisian women, armed with pikes and guns and knives, marched on the palace at Versailles. The women demanded an end to bread shortages and also forced the royal family to return to Paris, the site of popular rule. Louis submitted to the Declaration. The women's march was the first mass insurrection to use the language of popular sovereignty against a monarch.

Relative peace lasted for the next two years. During that time, the National Assembly wrote the Constitution of 1791 which established a constitutional monarchy. To deal with the financial crisis caused by the royal debt, the Assembly continued the economic policies advocated by Louis XVI's reformist ministers. These typically included protection of property plus trade freed of any restraints, which meant a banning of workers' union. The Assembly also confiscated and sold the property of the Catholic Church. Reaction came in a fury: the church launched a campaign against revolution and liberalism which lasted 100 years, and many aristocrats known as *emigres* left France to organize counter-revolution.

The Constituent Assembly dissolved itself in September 1791. Elections filled what was planned to be a permanent Legislative Assembly. But factionalism crippled the body for its one short year of life. Over the same period, women also attempted to raise their voices. Olympe de Gouges, a butcher's daughter, published a Declaration of the Rights of Women to extend further citizenship to women—a group relegated to stay home and raise children by many Enlightenment *philosophes* and political leaders. In 1792, events turned drastic: radicals from the working class organized themselves as the Paris Commune. In a campaign reportedly against counter-revolutionaries, the Commune killed about 1,200 people, mainly prisoners in Paris jails, in the "September Massacres." On the bloody heels, the Commune compelled the Assembly to decree universal a male suffrage and an election to a Convention to write a new constitution.

The Convention, named for the American revolutionary convention of 1787, declared France a republic. The second revolution was pushed forward radical Jacobins (The Mountain) and Parisian *sans culottes*—shopkeepers, artisans, and workers economically victimized by policies of the National Assembly. The two groups dominated the new assembly and voted an extreme action: the execution of Louis XVI.

Shaken, every major European ruler declared opposition to the revolution, and Prussia drove the French out of Belgium. By April 1793, the French Convention had declared war with Austria, Prussia, Great Britain, Spain, Sardinia, and Holland. The convention established the Committees of General Security and Public Safety. The latter, under the leadership of Danton, Carnot and Robespierre eventually enjoyed almost dictatorial power. The revolutionaries shifted the way they saw the revolution: it was not a struggle for national borders but for a new republican political and social order which was under siege by enemies. To protect the revolution extreme measures were justified. Thus, under the consequent Reign of Terror, in August, a levée en masse was issued which conscripted males into a citizen army—

Europe's first—and directed economic production for military purposes. In September the ceiling on prices which the *sans-culottes* had long demanded was instituted. As social turmoil continued, in October women were scapegoated and a campaign to suppress women began. Then in November the Convention outlawed the worship of God and tried to substitute a Cult of Reason. This alienated many Christians. Although some quasi-judicial bloodletting had already begun in the summer, executions increased from autumn of 1793 to the following summer. The Convention eliminated opposition through the execution of more than 25,000 people, including Olympe de Gouges and finally Robespierre himself.

The republic was created and France would never again remain under monarchy. Yet the Reign of Terror fostered a reaction that for a time stabilized the tumult of the revolution in France. In March 1795 the Convention concluded peace with Prussia and Spain and also beat back radicals at home, executing the leader Gracchus Babeuf, who advocated greater equality of property. France continued war with Austria and Great Britain, however, and the new and unstable Directory increasingly depended on the power of the army to govern the country.

The determination to defeat foreign enemies and export revolutionary ideals worked to the advantage of a brilliant young officer named Napoleon Bonaparte, who would turn the republican army into a instrument of European conquest in the era to come.

Into the nineteenth century, future monarchs and other royalists would attempt to reverse aspects of the revolution and restore the old order. But the step had been taken—a giant one—in the French Revolution, out of centuries of feudal, fixed hierarchies with aristocrats at the top and serfs at the bottom. With the French Revolution, the middle classes and the *sans-culottes* and peasants won a new fundamental share of power in determining the government, economy, and culture of western civilization.

Identifications

Identify each one of the following as used in the text. Refer to the text as necessary.

	Text page
parlements	351-352
Jacques Necker	352
cahiers de doléances	353
Tennis Court Oath	353
August 4, 1789	354
Olympe de Gouges	356, 364
Chapelier Law	358
assignats	358
émigrés	358, 359
sans-culottes	361, 363-365, 367
Paris Commune	361
The Mountain	361, 363
Maximilien Robespierre	363-365
Journey from St. Petersburg to Moscow	363
levée en masse	364
Society of Revolutionary Republican Women	364
dechristianization of France	364-365
Reign of Terror	363-365
enragés	365
Law of 22 Prairial	365

Map Exercise A

Locate each of the following on the accompanying map:

1. English Channel
2. Bay of Biscay
3. Mediterranean Sea
4. Cities of Metz, Lyons, Marseilles, Toulon, Paris, Verdun
5. Provinces of Burgundy and Brittany
6. Departments of Vendée and Gironde

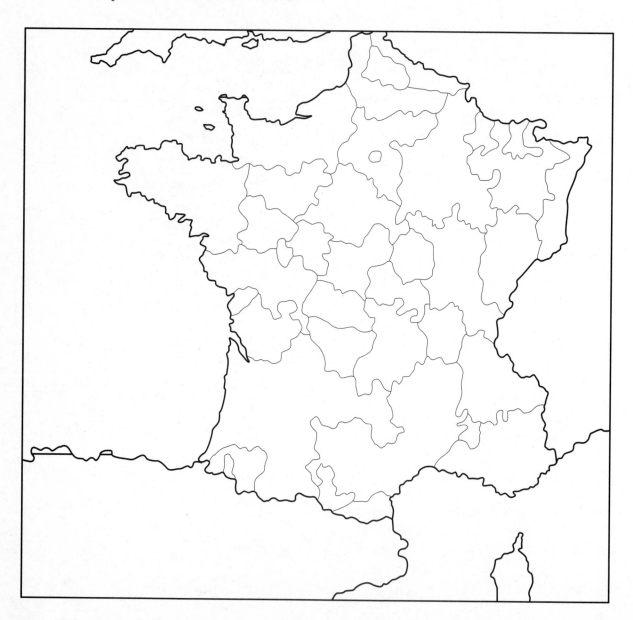

Map Exercise B

In the space below draw a free-hand map of modern France. Include at least three rivers, two mountain ranges, the capital city and all the countries that touch the borders of France. Don't forget Andorra.

Short-Answer Exercises

Multiple-Choice

_____1. The text notes that the French Revolution was caused by the fact that France:
  (a) gained new colonial territories as a result of her support of the American Revolution
  (b) was a rich nation with an impoverished government
  (c) was in debt way out of proportion when compared with other European states
  (d) all of these.

_____2. The budget presented by _____ did the most to incite opposition against the aristocracy and the government.
  (a) Étienne Charles Loménie de Brienne
  (b) René Maupeou
  (c) Jacques Necker
  (d) Charles Alexandre de Calonne

_____3. What is often considered as the document that put an end to the old regime in France was:
  (a) the *cahiers*
  (b) The Civil Constitution of the Clergy
  (c) The Declaration of the Rights of Man and the Citizen
  (d) The Tennis Court Oath

_____4. After the passage of the Civil Constitution of the Clergy, the Catholic Church in France was _____ to the French Revolution.
  (a) increasingly supportive
  (b) decreasingly supportive
  (c) openly opposed
  (d) none of these

_____5. Reacting to the French Revolution, Prime Minister Pitt of England:
  (a) sponsored pacifism among working-class reform groups in London
  (b) expanded the freedom of the press to allow lewd cartoons of French leaders
  (c) suppressed reform, making some political writing treasonable

_____6. In 1793 the Cathedral of Notre Dame became the:
  (a) headquarters of the Jacobin party
  (b) Temple of Virtue
  (c) prison of Marie Antoinette
  (d) Temple of Reason

_____7. The approximately 25,000 victims of the Reign of Terror were largely:
  (a) lower class
  (b) clergy
  (c) aristocracy
  (d) none of these

_____8. By the end of 1795 legislation in France regarding the status of women:
  (a) liberalized divorce procedures for them
  (b) supported their involvement in the political process
  (c) upgraded their status in the eyes of the Church
  (d) left them with somewhat less freedom than they enjoyed before 1789

_____9. The Thermidorean Constitution of the Year III (1795) required that members of the legislature be:
(a) married
(b) widowed
(c) female
(d) actually none of these choices is wholly accurate

_____10. Winning the leading voice in government by the end of the revolution were:
(a) the Thermidor Reaction Party, a group of nobles with private armies
(b) wealthy middle class and professional people
(c) the *sans-culottes* and peasants
(d) Jacobins from the French colonies

_____11. The Convention in the Republic phase of the revolution:
(a) abolished slavery in the French colonies
(b) admitted former slave Jean Baptiste Belley as a representative of Saint Domingue
(c) was named for the American Constitutional Convention
(d) all of the above

True/False

_____1. There were no casualties in the events surrounding the fall of the Bastille.

_____2. The "Great Fear" occurred in the summer of 1789 as a result of rumors of coming food shortages.

_____3. One of the major reasons for not immediately repudiating the French national debt was that much of it was owed to the bankers, merchants, commercial traders and other people in the Third Estate.

_____4. The new currency issued by the National Assembly near the end of 1790 was backed by lands confiscated from the aristocracy of France.

_____5. The 1792 massacre of persons in Paris jails by the Paris Commune came to be known as the "October Days."

_____6. An example of the effect the French Revolution was having on other European states was the burning of Voltaire's works by Catherine the Great.

_____7. For the new French Republic, Lazare Carnot, a prominent Jacobin, organized the first national citizen army in Europe.

_____8. The so-called *enragés* were a radical group of *sans-culottes* that urged greater price regulations and a more extreme policy of dechristianization.

_____9. The Thermidorean Reaction was chiefly supported by the aristocracy in combination with the *sans-culottes*.

_____10. One of the unanticipated results of the Thermidorean Reaction was a notable revival of Catholicism.

_____11. One goal which both Jacobins and *sans-culottes* agreed on was the abolition of private property and a nation with no small property owners.

Completion

1. In 1774 _____ became the king of France.

2. The question of _____ procedures remained an unresolved problem in 1788 and during the earliest meetings of the Estates-General.

3. The crowd of working people storming the Bastille July 14, 1789 wanted _____.

4. The 1791 Declaration of _____ was an effort by the kings of Austria and Prussia to protect the French royal family.

5. The most advanced and best organized political group of the National Constituent Assembly was the _____ .

6. The French Convention of 1792 actually took its name from the _____ of 1787.

7. The battle of _____ in 1792, which was won by the French Army, is often considered as the victory of democracy over aristocracy.

8. _____ took a position against the French Revolution in his work titled *Reflections on the Revolution in France.*

9. The more extreme aspect of the Thermidorean Reaction is known as the _____ .

10. The 1795 riots against the Convention brought attention to _____ .

For Further Consideration

1. Sum up the financial crisis the monarchy faced in France on the eve of the French Revolution. What caused the problem? What was the main stumbling block to a solution?

2. What were the policies of the National Constituent Assembly toward the Catholic Church? How would these policies "revolutionize" church-state relations throughout Europe?

3. What were at least three causes leading to the Reign of Terror? What, if anything in it, reminds you of any period in the American Revolution? If you like, write as if you were an enthusiastic *sans-culotte* or a Jacobin in The Mountain.

4. Describe the Thermidorean Reaction. Why should these events be considered an important parts of the era of the French Revolution?

5. The French Revolution is often characterized as the beginning of the end of the old regime in Europe as well as a sign of things to come in the nineteenth and twentieth centuries. Comment on this statement using appropriate examples as necessary.

6. Describe at least one action in the French Revolution where a woman or women played dramatic or leading roles. How do you account for such boldness at a time when the *philosophes* said a woman's place was at home with children? What, if anything, about this reminds you of any situation today?

7. Optional: The text says that the Jacobins and *sans-culottes* shared a common vision of France to become a nation of small property owners. How did the Revolution change the way French society regarded wealth and property from aristocratic birth? From middle class commerce? From peasants? City workers?

Answers

Multiple-Choice

Text page

1. B 351
2. C 352
3. C 355
4. C 358
5. C 363
6. D 364
7. A 365
8. D 366
9. D 366
10. B 365
11. D 361, 366

True/False

1. F 354
2. F 354
3. T 358
4. F 358
5. F 361
6. T 363
7. T 364
8. T 365
9. F 365-366
10. T 366
11. F 361

Completion

1. Louis XVI 351
2. voting/representation 353
3. weapons/armaments 353
4. Pillniz 359
5. Jacobins 359
6. American Constitutional Convention 361
7. Valmy 361
8. Edmund Burke 362
9. White Terror 365
10. Napoleon Bonaparte 368

20
The Age of Napoleon and the Triumph of Romanticism

Commentary

This chapter deals with the period from about 1797 to 1820 and especially with the figure of Napoleon Bonaparte: his rise to power, his campaigns that conquered most of Europe, his final defeat and the settlement reached at the Congress of Vienna. It goes on to discuss Romanticism, a new intellectual movement which spread throughout Europe.

The government of the Directory represented a society of recently rich and powerful people whose chief goal was to perpetuate their own rule. Their chief opposition came from the royalists, who won a majority in the elections of 1797. With the aid of Napoleon, the anti-monarchist Directory staged a *coup d'état* and put their own supporters into the legislature. In the meantime, Napoleon was crushing Austrian and Sardinian armies in Italy. An invasion of Egypt, however, was a failure. Upon his return in 1799, Napoleon led a new *coup d'état* and issued the Constitution of th e Year VIII, which established the rule of one man and may be regarded as the end of the revolution in France.

Bonaparte soon achieved peace with Austria and Britain and was equally effective in restoring order at home. In 1801, he reached an agreement with the pope. The agreement restored the status of the Roman Catholic Church as the official French religion. But the state took supremacy over the church and subordinated the church to the state, including requiring religious tolerance. In 1802, a plebiscite appointed him consul for life and obtained full power from a new constitution. A general codification of laws called the Napoleonic Code soon followed. The Code abolished serfdom, hereditary social distinctions, medieval urban guilds and oligarchies, and subordinated the church to the state, including requiring religious tolerance. In 1804, Napoleon made himself emperor Napoleon I with yet another constitution. In his decade as emperor (1804–1814) Napoleon conquered most of Europe. He could put as many as 700,000 men under arms at any one time and depended on mobility and timing to achieve the destruction of the enemy army.

The chapter now discusses Napoleon's impressive victory at Austerlitz (1805), setback at Trafalgar (1805) and defeat of the Prussian and Russians which resulted in the Treaty of Tilsit (1807). Napoleon organized Europe into the French Eire and a number of satellite states over which ruled the members of his family. To defeat the British, Napoleon devised the Continental System, which aimed at cutting off British trade with the European continent. However, Britain's other markets (in the Americas and the eastern Mediterranean), plus smuggling, enabled the British economy to survive.

Napoleon's conquests stimulated liberalism and nationalism. As it became increasingly clear that Napoleon's policies were to benefit France rather than Europe, the conquered states and peoples became restive. In 1806, a general guerrilla rebellion—a new style of warfare relying on ordinary citizens—began in Spain (over Napoleon's deposition of the Bourbon dynasty) and in 1810, the Russian withdrew from the Continental System. The invasion of Russia that followed along with the disastrous retreat from Moscow in the winter of 1812-1813 exposed French weaknesses. A powerful coalition defeated the French in the "Battle of Nations" (1813). In 1814 the allied army took Paris and Napoleon abdicated, going to the island of Elba.

The Congress of Vienna met from September 1814 to November 1815. The arrangements were essentially made by four great powers: Britain, Austria, Prussia, and Russia; the key person in achieving agreement was British foreign secretary Castlereagh. The victors agreed that no single state should dominate Europe. Proceedings were interrupted by Napoleon's return in March 1815. They soon defeated him at Waterloo. The episode hardened the peace settlement for France, but Congress settled difficult problems in a reasonable way. No general war occurred for a century.

A new intellectual movement known as Romanticism emerged as a reaction against the Enlightenment. The Age of Romanticism was roughly 1780-1830. Romantic thinkers challenged the Enlightenment *philsophes'* emphasis on math and reason and instead insisted on the role of imagination, feelings, and and inspiration as tools for knowledge. Romantic religious thinkers appealed to the inner emotion of humankind for the foundation of religion. Methodist teachings, for example, emphasized inward, heartfelt religion and the possibility of Christian perfection in the is life. Romanticism glorified both the individual person and individual cultures. German writers such as Herder and the Grimm brothers went in search of their own past and revived German folk culture. Romantic ideas, then, made a major contribution to the emergence of a nationalism by emphasizing the worth of each separate people.

Identifications

Identify each one of the following as used in the text. Refer to the text as necessary.

	Text Page
Abbé Siéyès	372
Consulate government	372
Treaty of Amiens	372-374
Organic Articles of 1802	373
Napoleonic Code	373-375
Horatio Nelson	374
Continental System	374-375
Baron von Stein	375
General Kutuzov and "scorched Earth"	380
Battle of Borodino	380
Treaty of Chaumont	380
The Hundred Days	382
Waterloo	383
Holy Alliance	383
Quadruple Alliance	383
Romantics	383-388
Émile	385
Social Contract	385
"categorical imperative"	385
Ode on Intimations of Immortality	386
Faust	387
Methodism	387-388
The Genius of Christianity	388
thesis, antithesis, synthesis	388
Johann Gottfried Herder	388

Map Exercise A

Locate each of the following on the accompanying map:

1.	Corsica	6.	Marseilles
2.	Ottoman Empire	7.	Berlin
3.	Versailles	8.	Vienna
4.	Island of Elba	9.	Warsaw
5.	Paris	10.	Moscow

Locate each of these battles:

1.	Trafalgar	6.	Borodino
2.	Austerlitz	7.	Dresden
3.	Jena	8.	Leipzig
4.	Friedland	9.	Waterloo
5.	Wagram		

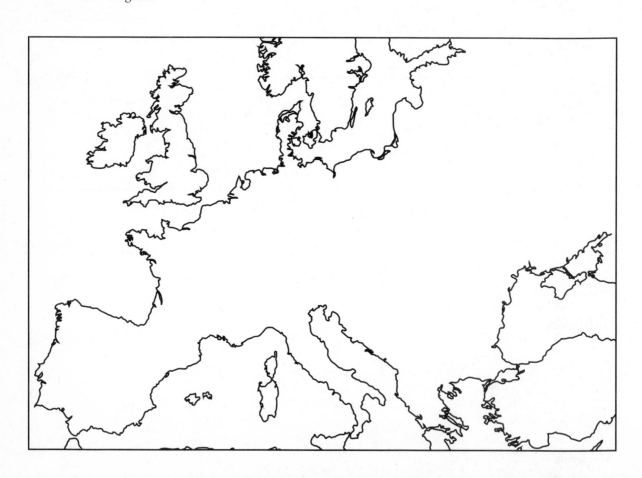

Map Exercise B

Outline the borders of the modern states of Europe. Mark the extent of the French Imperium as it appeared in 1812.

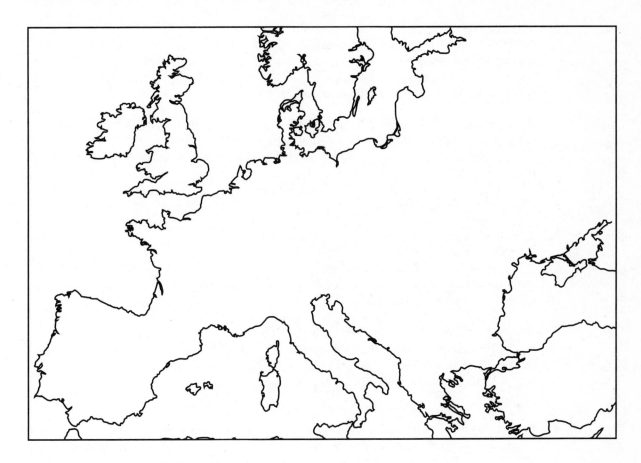

Short-Answer Exercises

Multiple-Choice

_____1. The Napoleonic Constitution of 1799:
   (a) was outwardly dictatorial
   (b) was modeled after that of the United States
   (c) contained a suggestion of democratic principles and republican theories
   (d) was none of these.

_____2. With the Napoleonic Code of 1804:
   (a) fathers had extensive control over their families
   (b) females could now receive inheritances
   (c) labor unions were forbidden
   (d) all of these were part of the Code.

_____3. One of the reasons Napoleon established the Bonapartist dynasty in 1804 was:
(a) the need to publicly demonstrate supremacy over the Church in France
(b) the need to demonstrate supremacy over the Pope
(c) that it would create a recognizable heir to his throne
(d) he believed it was necessary for him to get into a good college

_____4. The Continental System:
(a) was an effective weapon against British trade
(b) encouraged smuggling
(c) prevented smuggling
(d) created a free trade zone throughout Europe

_____5. Which of the following would be associated with the reforms of the Napoleonic Code as it affected France and much of Europe under Napoleon?
(a) workers' organizations were forbidden, but peasants were freed from serfdom
(b) privilege by birth was abolished
(c) privilege by ownership or property was safeguarded
(d) all of the above

_____6. Rebellion against French rule in Spain came from the:
(a) nobility and upper clergy
(b) peasants and monastic leaders
(c) upper classes
(d) peasants and the lower clergy

_____7. Napoleon's Concordat (agreement) with the Catholic Church produced:
(a) the Church's agreement to give up claims to property lost in the revolution
(b) the restoration of the Pope's power to crown kings
(c) an annulment of Napoleon's childless marriage
(d) all of the above

_____8. Prussia's social reforms, while imitating France, faced problems in:
(a) Junkers who continued to take feudal duties from peasants who stayed on their land
(b) a population explosion which enlarged the country's landless labor force
(c) neither of these
(d) both of these

_____9. Friedrich Schlegel's *Lucinde* (1799) shocked many contemporaries because:
(a) it openly discussed sexual activity
(b) it showed a woman in equal status to a man
(c) it did not cater to existing prejudices against women
(d) of all of these

_____10. The idea that religion is a great and emotional experience would be least associated with:
(a) Immanuel Kant
(b) Friedrich Schleiermacher
(c) John Wesley
(d) François René de Chateaubriand

_____11. The Grand Army of Napoleon drew power from:
(a) enormous numbers of up to 700,000 soldiers
(b) guerrilla tactics to fight in small, hit-and-run bands
(c) a "scorched earth" practice of wiping out everything in its path of retreat
(d) its slow chewing up of the enemy

True/False

_____1. With the complete support of the government at Paris, Napoleon negotiated the Treaty of Campo Formio (October 1797) which took the Austrian Empire out of the First Coalition.

_____2. The poets Wordsworth and Coleridge saw childhood as the bright period of creative imagination.

_____3. The Treaty of Tilsit between Russia's Tzar Alexander and Napoleon Bonaparte cost Prussia dearly.

_____4. The German political leaders von Stein and von Hardenburg generally supported democratic reform in Prussia.

_____5. Sir Arthur Wellesley commanded British forces during the Peninsular War in Spain.

_____6. Napoleon's Grand Army, which invaded Russia in 1812, lost 150,000 of its 600,000 soldiers to the Russian winter and Russian "scorched earth" tactics.

_____7. Napoleon was defeated by the combined armies of the other European states in 1813 at Leipzig.

_____8. In *Émile* Rousseau urged the importance of strict upbringing of children so that they might later flourish as adults.

_____9. In his *The Genius of Christianity* François Chateaubriand described his conversion from Judaism to Methodism.

_____10. Johann Gottfried Herder stressed the acceptability of universal culture and the common humanity of the entire planet.

Completion

1. After Napoleon's defeat of the Austrians in October 1797, France's only real enemy was _____ .

2. The execution of the _____ put an end to royalist plots against Napoleon's government.

3. Probably the battle at _____ against the combined forces of Russia and Austria was Napoleon's greatest victory.

4. *The Third of May, 1808,* a painting by _____, is one of the earliest paintings to celebrate the impassioned civilian guerrilla.

5. French representative _____ led the Congress of Vienna away from new war.

6. _____ wrote *The Prelude,* an autobiographical story of his becoming a poet.

7. Along with Coleridge, Blake, Shelley, and Wordsworth, _____ was another lead-
    ing English Romantic poet famous for his rebellious politics and love life.

8. _____, the masterwork of Goethe, is the story of a man, who, weary of life, made
    a pact with the devil.

9. _____ argued that particularly strong rulers can impose their will on others.

10. The influential German philosopher _____ saw history as the movement of ideas
    in a process of conflict, contradiction, and then resolution (also known as *dialectics*).

For Further Consideration

1. Explain the rise of Napoleon Bonaparte. Can this be considered a classic example of man making
history, or were conditions favorable to the emergence of a "Napoleon-like" leader?

2. How did France under Napoleon actually control Europe? Was there a common theme to all of Napoleon's actions during this era? Why were the European states for so long unable to organize against the French threat?

3. Discuss the circumstances that brought about the Congress of Vienna. What were the major successes and failures of the meeting? Are there any long-term, historical factors to be associated with the Congress of Vienna? If so, what are they?

4. Define Romanticism. Focus on one aspect of the text (e.g. literature, religion, history, art.) Give an example of a writer or artist or work or movement to illustrate your definition.

or

Which approach to life works for you—that of the Romantic or the ways of the Rational Enlightenment? What features of either approach do you find useful?

5. You have surveyed three revolutions—the Glorious, the American, and the French. Write briefly what you see that they had in common.

Answers

Multiple-Choice

		Text page
1.	C	372
2.	D	373
3.	C	373
4.	B	375
5.	D	373
6.	D	377-378
7.	A	373
8.	D	375
9.	D	387
10.	A	385
11.	D	380

True/False

1.	F	372
2.	T	386
3.	T	374
4.	F	375
5.	T	375
6.	T	380
7.	T	380
8.	F	385
9.	F	388
10.	F	388

Completion

1.	Great Britain	372
2.	Duke of Enghien	373
3.	Austerlitz	374
4.	Francisco Goya	377
5.	Talleyrand	382
6.	William Wordsworth	386
7.	Lord Byron	386
8.	*Faust*	387
9.	J.G. Fichte	388
10.	Georg W. E. Hegel	388

21

The Conservative Order and the Challenges of Reform (1815–1832)

Commentary

The defeat of Napoleon and the diplomatic settlement of the Congress of Vienna restored the conservative political and social order in Europe. This chapter deals with the confrontation of this conservative order with potential sources of unrest found in the forces of liberalism, nationalism and popular sovereignty. The chapter surveys Russia, Austria, Prussia, Great Britain, France, Greece, Haiti and Latin America, although not necessarily in the order discussed below.

Tsar Alexander I's development as a ruler reflected the turn of eastern European states from Enlightened Absolutism to rigid conservatism. His reformist tendencies waned after he led Russia into war with Napoleon in 1807. However, military defeats convinced him that reform was necessary. Yet by 1812, censorship had become the order of the day; there was little toleration of political opposition or criticism.

The Austrian government could make no serious compromises with the programs of liberalism and nationalism, which would have meant the probable dissolution of the empire. The Austrian statesman, Metternich, epitomized conservatism. In the immediate post-war years, he was primarily concerned with preventing movements toward constitutionalism in the German states.

In Great Britain, unemployment led to demands for the reform of Parliament. For a time, repression brought calm, but in 1817, the Coercion Acts were passed and in 1819 the Six Act was passed. Among other things, they outlawed labor unions and large unauthorized public meetings. These attempted to remove the instruments of agitation from the hands of radical leaders and to provide the authorities with new powers.

The Bourbon monarchy was restored to France. Louis XVIII attempted to pursue a policy of mild accommodation with the liberals, supported by the restoration constitution called the Charter. In 1829, the assassination of his nephew persuaded Louis to take a harder line.

Foreign policy issues were worked out through congresses, or later, more informal consultations in a system known as the Concert of Europe. At Aix-la-Chapelle in 1818, Tsar Alexander I suggested that the Quadruple Alliance (Russia, Austria, Prussia and Great Britain) agree to uphold the borders and existing governments of all European countries. Britain contended that the Quadruple Alliance was intended only to prevent future French aggression and flatly rejected the proposal. The text then sketches the revolution in Spain and Italy in 1820. The final result was that Britain withdrew from continental affairs, but the others agreed to support Austrian intervention in Italy and French intervention in Spain. The revolution which took place in Greece in 1821 was part of a larger problem: the weakness of the Ottoman Empire. The conflicting interests of the major powers prevented any direct intervention in Greece for several years, but finally Britain, France and Russia supported the Greeks. A Treaty of

London in 1830 declared Greece an independent kingdom. The wars of Napoleon also sparked independence movements from European domination in Latin America. Haiti achieved independence from France through a slave revolt led by Toussaint L'Ouverture. The efforts of Jose de San Martin (Peru and Chile), Simon Bolivar (Venezuela), and Bernardo O'Higgins (Chile) are also discussed, as well as events in Mexico and Brazil.

Nineteenth-century liberals wanted to limit the arbitrary power of the government against the persons and the property of individual citizens. Liberalism was often complementary to nationalism in Germany, Greece and the Austrian empire. During the 1820s, Russia took the lead in suppressing liberal and nationalistic tendencies. Nicholas I ascended to the throne in 1825 and soon put down the Decembrist Revolt. Nicholas I was the most extreme of the nineteenth-century autocrats. He embraced a program called Official Nationalism which had the slogan "Orthodoxy, Autocracy and Nationalism." The program alienated serious Russian intellectual life from the tsarist government. In response to an uprising in Poland in 1830, Nicholas sent in troops and declared Poland to be an integral part of the Russian empire.

Charles X, an ultra royalist, succeeded to the French throne in 1824 and tried to roll back as much of the revolution as possible. When elections in 1830 resulted in a stunning victory for the liberals, Charles issued the Four Ordinances (July 1830) which amounted to a royal coup d'etat. Rioting broke out in Paris and Charles abdicated. Louis Philippe was proclaimed the new monarch and politically his rule was more liberal than the restoration government. But socially, the revolution on 1830 proved quite conservative and little sympathy was displayed for the lower classes: violent uprisings continued to occur.

The July Days in Paris started an independence movement in Belgium. The former Austrian Netherlands had been merged with Holland in 1815, but the upper classes in Belgium had never reconciled themselves to rule by a country with a different language, religion and economic life. After defeating Dutch troops, Belgian revolutionaries wrote a constitution which was promulgated in 1831. Thanks to the efforts of Britain's Lord Palmerston, the other European powers recognized Belgium as an independent and neutral state.

In Britain, the forces of conservatism and reform made accommodations with each other. Several factors made this possible: a large commercial and industrial class, a tradition of liberal Whig aristocrats, and a strong respect for civil liberties. The chapter ends by discussing reforms such as the Catholic Emancipation Act (1829) and the Great Reform Bill of 1832.

Identifications

Identify each one of the following as used in the text. Refer to the text as necessary.

	text page
nationhood	391
Liberal	391-392
the German Confederation	393
"War of Liberation"	393
Prince Metternich	393
tercentenary of Luther's Ninety-Five Theses	394
Karl Sand	394
Carlsbad Decrees	394
Combination Acts of 1799	394
"Peterloo" Massacre and the Six Acts	395
ultraroyalism	395
Quadruple Alliance	396
Congress of Troppau	396
Treaty of London	397
Karageorge	397
Toussaint L'Ouverture and Jean Jacques Dessalines	397, 409-410
creole elites	398-399
junta	399
Simón Bolivar	399
José María Morelos y Pavón	400

Map Exercise A

On the accompanying map outline the early eighteenth-century boundaries of Mexico and the states of Central and South America.

Map Exercise B

Locate each of the following on this map of the Caribbean Basin.

Florida
Bahamas
Cuba
Island of Hispaniola
Haiti
Jamaica

Puerto Rico
Panama
Venezuela
Mexico
Barbados
Curaçao

Do your own research, using maps from throughout the text, and also see page vi of this guide for additional references.

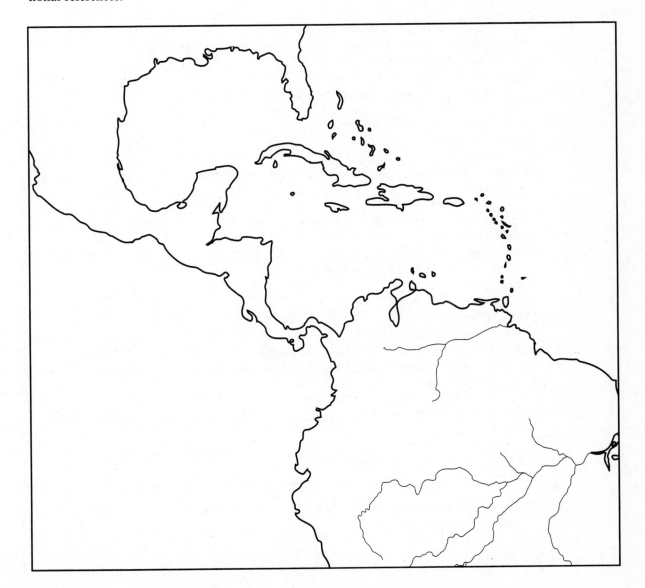

Short-Answer Exercises

Multiple-Choice

_____1. The real goal of this era's political liberals was:
(a) mass democracy
(b) political reforms and greater representation based on property ownership
(c) free education for all
(d) the end of poverty

_____2. Political liberalism of the early 1800s often accompanied:
(a) economic liberalism, especially an enthusiasm for free trade
(b) deep respect for poor people
(c) Roman Catholicism

_____ 3. Which of the following occurred in England?
(a) liberal student groups and the Carlsbad Decrees that outlawed them
(b) a White Terror by royalists
(c) the Protocol of Troppau against revolutions
(d) clash between troops and reformers called "Peterloo"

_____4. The Concert of Europe was:
(a) a radical political party
(b) the dream child of the Russian Tsar
(c) a symphony orchestra sponsored by the poet Lord Byron
(d) none of these

_____5. Alexander I's reign (1801–1825) can be considered as:
(a) liberal throughout
(b) conservative throughout
(c) initially liberal and later conservative
(d) none of these

_____6. European interest in the Ottoman Empire stemmed from:
(a) the desire for commercial access
(b) direct competition between Austria and Russia
(c) a desire to have access to the shrines in the Holy Land
(d) all of these factors

_____7. Early in the nineteenth century, _____ assumed the role of protector of Serbia.
(a) Austria
(b) England
(c) France
(d) Russia

_____8. The Decembrist movement in Russia wanted to achieve all of the following except:
(a) constitutional government
(b) election of Tsars
(c) Constantine to be Tsar
(d) reforms

_____9. The Four Ordinances issued by Charles X of France:
  (a) restricted freedom of the press
  (b) restricted the franchise to only the wealthiest people in the country
  (c) brought a strong reaction throughout much of French society
  (d) all of these

_____10. Britain's Great Reform Bill of 1832 achieved:
  (a) new rights for women
  (b) a reduction in the property requirements for voting
  (c) better representation for a wider variety of propertied people
  (d) a social safety net for the poor

_____11. The July Revolution of 1830:
  (a) came after France defeated Algeria and started an empire in North Africa
  (b) increased power to Paris' lower classes
  (c) ended influence-peddling and other government corruption
  (d) all of the above

True/False

_____1. In the first quarter of the nineteenth century, there was no formulaic way that nationalism and liberalism related to each other.

_____2. The Combination Acts outlawing labor unions were passed as a result of a December 1811 mass protest near London at Spa Fields.

_____3. An important factor in repressive measures taken by Louis XVIII of France can be found in the 1820 assassination of the Duke de Berri, a man in line for the French throne.

_____4. Without question, Tsar Alexander I of Russia is considered the chief architect of the post-Vienna world.

_____5. Creole leaders in Latin America could be said to have developed a reform program based upon Enlightenment ideas and those associated with the American Revolution.

_____6. Let by the Creole monarchist, Hidalgo y Costilla, Mexico was the first area in Latin America to reject independence from Spain.

_____7. Simon Bolivar's fight for a republican Venezuela had help from newly independent Haiti.

_____8. By the declaration of Nicholas I's Organic Statute Poland became an integral part of the Russian empire.

_____9. The Greek revolution of 1821 attracted liberal literary figures, like Lord Byron, by aiming to return democracy to the land of its birth.

_____10. In 1832 England's Great Reform Bill extended the electoral franchise to all males over the age of twenty-one.

_____11. The British abolitionist movement attacked the slave trade but not slave ownership.

Completion

1. It is clear today that a common _____ is required as a basic building block for the

   establishment of a new nation.

2. Many of the ideas of nineteenth-century liberals can be attributed to the writers of the

   _____ .

3. During this period German student associations were called _____ .

4. _____, brother of the king executed in the French Revolution, became the first king of France after the abdication of Napoleon.

5. The document which declared that stable governments could intervene in other countries to restore a conservative order was the _____ .

6. Although established as a dictator, the hero of Chilean independence was _____ .

7. The French city of _____ witnessed more than one serious workers' strike during the 1830s.

8. The first king of an independent Belgium was _____ .

9. _____ gained independence in 1839, partly on the condition that it remain neutral among France, England and other countries.

10. The 1829 _____ Act passed by the British Parliament was directly related to the Irish Question.

For Further Consideration

1. What challenges in German society did liberals face as they sought political power? What was one key goal of German liberals? What role did the German student movement play?

2. A slave revolt began in Haiti's movement for independence in the age of the French and American Revolutions and the Enlightenment. Using your imagination, name at least two ideas which the Haitians and revolutionaries overseas may have shared in common. What do you imagine motivated Haiti to give aid to Venezuela's liberation?

3. Sum up the role and motives played by the creole elites in the revolutionary movements in Latin America in this period. Choose one country—e.g. Brazil, Argentina, Mexico, or Venezuela—and describe several features of creole participation. What is similar to European liberal movements of the time?

4. Throughout the nineteenth century, Russia was considered the most conservative state compared to others in Europe. What causes do you see for this? If it helps, review economics, geography, religion, the military and the government of Russia for answers.

5. What factors allowed Britain to be a leading test ground for European liberal thought and activities?

Answers

Multiple Choice

Text page

1. B 391-392
2. A 392
3. D 395
4. D 396
5. B 400-401
6. D 397
7. D 397
8. B 400
9. D 402
10. C 406
11. A 403

True/False

1. T 391
2. F 394
3. T 395
4. F 393-396
5. T 399
6. F 399-400
7. T 399
8. T 402
9. T 396
10. F 406
11. T 409

Completion

1. language 391
2. Enlightenment 391
3. *Bruchenschaften* 394
4. Louis XVIII 395
5. Protocol of Troppau 396
6. Bernardo O'Higgins 399
7. Lyons 403
8. Leopold of Saxe-Coburg 404
9. Belgium 404
10. Catholic Emancipation 404-405

22
Economic Advance and
Social Unrest (1830-1850)

Commentary

This chapter traces the growth of industrialism in early nineteenth-century Europe and its social repercussions. These included people moving in great numbers to the cities, poor living conditions there, more-mechanized factories, debates over economic and social theories explaining these developments, and political agitation. The chapter concludes by describing how tension broke into a wave of revolutions throughout Europe in 1848. Liberals and nationalists led the revolts. All were crushed.

The chapter begins with the industrial revolution. The earliest advances had started in textiles in eighteenth-century Britain, and by 1850, further successes pushed the country's economy a generation ahead of its continental competitors. Indeed, the wealth Britain acquired through its multiple industries of textiles, ironmaking, shipbuilding, and other production allowed its owners to dominate the world scene for the entire nineteenth century.

Technology and social changes moved together. The 1830s and 1840s were the age of railroad construction, trains being the most dramatic application of the steam engine. The building of railways boosted demand for iron, steel, and workers. The population explosion of the eighteenth century continued and the labor force also grew diverse, including miners, factory workers, urban artisans, cottage-industry craftspeople, rural peddlers, farm workers, and railroad avvies. Workers filled the cities which grew faster than housing, sewers, lighting, and food supplies. Europe also suffered the century's worst agricultural disaster in the Irish potato famine of 1845-1847. A half million Irish starved to death and hundreds of thousands emigrated.

Under all these pressures, the two main groups of urban workers—the artisans and factory workers—endured a process of proletarianization: they lost their medieval tradition of owning their own tools and controlling their trades through guilds. Instead, they became dependent on the factory owners for tools and equipment, they worked for wages at a pace to suit machines, and they faced threats and punishment while they labored. They also could face unemployment, wretched living places, severe food shortages and other brutalities of poverty.

By the late 1830s, the British working classes turned to direct political activity and they pushed a reform program known as Chartism. Chartists advocated for universal male suffrage, the secret ballot, the abolition of property qualifications for members of Parliament, and other political reforms. As a national movement Chartism failed, in part because members split between pacifist and violent factions. But Chartism was the first large-scale English political movement organized by the working class, and it set an example for workers on the continent.

The chapter then focuses on other social effect of industrialism. In particular, the working-class family structure changed. Wheras formerly economic life was based in the home, now work was done in factories or elsewhere. The family, once a production unit, now became a consumer unit (aside from continuing to produce children). Women worked outside the home, receiving lower wages than men. The employment of children further broke the working-class family. The English Factory Act of 1833 regulated such employment, prohibiting work by children under nine, reducing the workday of children under thirteen to nine hours and further requiring two hours of daily schooling at the factory owner's expense. A year later, in 1834, a new Poor Law toughened work life for poor adults by mandating that the people could only receive public assistance by entering the workhouses, where conditions and work were intentionally harsh under the idea the pain would motivate the poor.

Police and new-style prisons were an innovation to contain the poorer classes of criminals. The ruling classes created police forces separate from the army in 1828 in Paris and London. Prisons also changed through a reform movement based on the theories that character flaws created criminals, and thus, conditions in prisons should force inmates to confront their "bad" tendencies. The results included models like those in Auburn, New York. In Auburn, prisoners were isolated at night but worked by day together in rehabilitative projects. An opposite model, Pentonville near London. Here inmates lived completely alone, having to wear masks when together and never being allowed to speak. France's version of extreme repressions was the notorious Devil's Island off the coast of South America. There prisoners judges incorrigible were locked away.

The chapter discusses the intellectual developments which influenced social policy. Classical economists such as Thomas Malthus and David Ricardo were leaders. Disciples of Adam Smith, they believed in competition for business. They also maintained that the misery of the working class could not be improved. Malthus claimed that populations naturally grow more rapidly than food supplies, and the best solution was to allow this. Workers would stop having children they could not feed. Malthus opposed raising wages or allowing trade unions. Employers welcomed his views. Closely related to the classical economists were the British ultilitarians led by Jeremy Bentham who defined utility to mean "the greatest good for the greatest number" as a guide for social policy. The classical economists and utilitarians or their followers actually wrote much of the legislation around child labor, prisons, and workhouses.

The period also produced an opposing socialist movement. Socialists applauded the productive capacity of industrialism but criticized the mismangement, low wages, and inequitable distribution of goods and wealth. Socialists wanted society to function as a humane community rather than an aggregate of atomistic, selfish individuals. Early socialists were sometimes called utopian socialists, after humanist Thomas More's famous book of 1516 *Utopia*. Like More, these nineteenth-century socialists proposed ideal communities often based on communal property or other mono-capitalistic values. Some proposed including looser family ties and sexual free love.

Another movement, anarchists, opposed any cooperation with organized industries or governments. Some anarchists, such as August Blanqui, were against capitalism and other, like Pierre Proudhon's, supported small businesses. Blanqui also supported terror and Proudhon supported peaceful tactics.

The ideas of Karl Marx were debated along with those of other thinkers. But Marxism distinguished itself by its claim to treat history as a science, as in *The Communist Manifesto*. Marxism also attracted interest with its theory of class conflict, and with its utopian message that history would inevitably move towards a struggle where the proletariat would revolt, abolish private property, and become free, and thus would free all humanity. Marx believed that class conflict in the nineteenth century had reached the point where the final clash between those owning the industries (the bourgeoisie) and those who owned nothing but who worked for the owners (the proletariat) was soon to come, and the property-less and classless society would follow.

In the 1830s and 1840s the working classes were not alone in being restive. The middle classes grew impatient for more political power. Liberals and nationals among them led actions for civil liberties, for better representative government, and for an unregulated economy. At critical moments, to put pressure on their monarchs, leaders appealed for support from the urban and working class. Out of these relationships, in 1848 a wave of liberal and national revolutions erupted across the continent. The political outbreak swept through France, Austria-Hungary, Italy, Prussia and the German states. The 1848 revolutions were stunning because never in a single year had Europe known so many uprisings. They all were suppressed, and conservatives seized power.

After 1848 the middle class ceased to be revolutionary and became increasingly concerned with protecting its property. It particularly feared radical movements associated with socialism and Marxism.

Identifications

Identify each one of the following as used in the text. Refer to the text as necessary.

	text page
proletarianization	416
confection	416
Chartism	416-417
English Factory Act	418
"bobbies"	420
John Howard, Elizabeth Fry and Charles Lucas	420
Pentonville Prison	420
Iron Law of Wages	421
Anti-Corn Law League	421
Poor Law of 1834	421
Utopian Socialism	422
Auguste Blanqui and Pierre Joseph Proudhon	423
dictatorship of the proletariat	424
The Communist Manifesto	424

Map Exercise A

Outline the boundaries of the European states at the mid-nineteenth-century point. Mark the urban centers of revolution for the 1848-1849 period.

Do your own research, using maps from the text (p. 379 and 381 may be useful) and also see page vi of this guide for additional references.

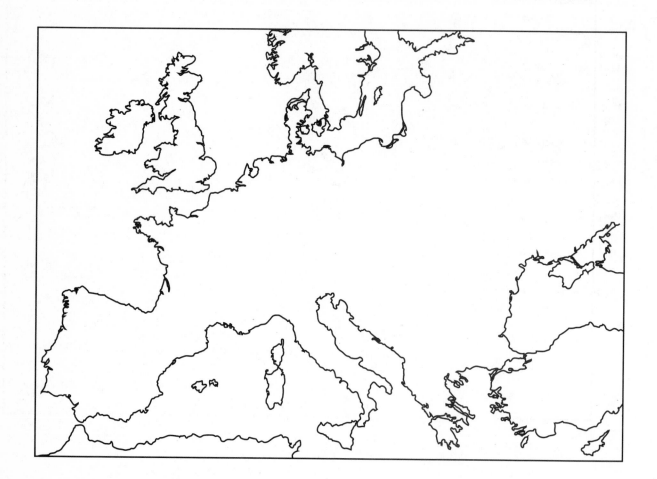

Map Exercise B

Draw a map outlining the contemporary boundaries of France. Include the major geographical features, rivers, mountain ranges, etc. Include water boundaries and mark the borders with other European states.

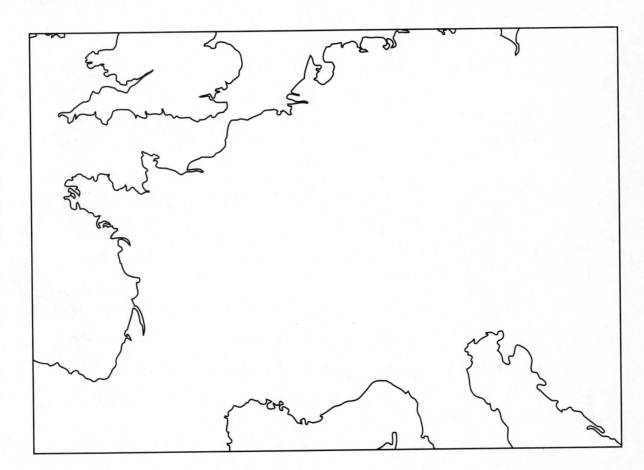

Short-Answer Exercises

Multiple-Choice

_____1. Which of the following did not contribute to the industrial strength of Great Britain in the nineteenth century?
(a) natural resources
(b) economic depression in the 1830s
(c) adequate financial resources
(d) French markets weakened by revolution and wars

_____2. The largest railroad network in Europe before 1850 could be found in:
(a) England
(b) France
(c) Belgium
(d) Germany

_____3. Which of the following groups would not be considered a part of the early nineteenth-century labor force?
(a) skilled urban artisans and factory workers
(b) shopkeepers and inventors
(c) farm workers and countryside peddlers
(d) the working poor

_____4. Which of the following would not be considered part of the Chartist reform program?
(a) women's rights
(b) annual election of the House of Commons
(c) universal manhood suffrage
(d) salaries for Members of Parliament

_____5. Which of the following is the most correct statement about the process of industrialization as it affected women?
(a) women could now become the head of households
(b) women would have less control over family finances
(c) there were choices for women in work and marriage
(d) none of these is correct

_____6. One reason for the repeal of the British Corn Laws was:
(a) both rich and poor wanted corn from American farms
(b) lobbying by British manufacturers
(c) attacks on cornfields by Chartist workers
(d) a glut of potatoes and corn in Ireland

_____7. Which of the following was not a major source of Karl Marx's ideas?
(a) German Hegelianism
(b) his family's Judeo-Lutheran background
(c) French socialism
(d) British economic theory

_____8. Demands of French women's groups during the revolution of 1848 included all of the following except:
(a) freedom from child-rearing duties
(b) civic and property rights
(c) educational opportunities
(d) the right to vote

_____9. _____ led the Hungarian independence movement against the Hapsburgs in 1848–1850.
(a) Alphonse Lamartine
(b) Friedrich Engels
(c) Louis Blanc
(d) Louis Kossuth

_____10. Which of the following is not associated with the conservative reaction to the revolutions of 1848?
(a) Giuseppe Garibaldi
(b) General Cavaignac
(c) General Radetzky
(d) General Windischgrätz

_____11. *The Communist Manifesto* by Marx and Engels said that:
(a) history is humankind's struggle to produce goods and other needs for life
(b) the dictatorship of the *proletariat* was aimed at lazy workers
(c) the middle class was the key class
(d) class conflict died withthe French Revolution

True/False

_____1. By the middle of the nineteenth century England was the most populous country of Europe.

_____2. The most dramatic application of steam technology was in the growth of railroads in Europe, and railroads epitomized the industrial economy.

_____3. Among the Chartist reforms were demands for salaries for elected members of the House of Commons.

_____4. Though there were many eighteenth-century textile-related inventions, it was the mechanization of weaving that had the greatest effect on the methods of work.

_____5. The most likely job for a poor English woman was working the land.

_____6. Police—a permanent force distinct from an army—did not exist until the early nineteenth century.

_____7. Unlike New York's Auburn prison, the nineteenth-century Philadelphia prison system called for the complete isolation of the prisoners from each other, following English and French models.

_____8. The major European utopian socialists expected their reforming ideas to prevail as a result of mass revolutions by the workers.

_____9. While no single factor caused the upheavals of 1848, widespread food shortages and unemployment and wretched living conditions in the cities all contributed.

_____10. Feminist efforts in France during the mid-century revolutions there led to near-full acceptance of their agenda for education, economic security and limited voting rights.

_____11. Socialists wanted society to function as a humane community, not a collection of atomisitc, selfish individuals.

_____12. Britain's Parliament reduced the working day to ten hours in 1847.

Completion

1. By the middle of the nineteenth century half the population of _____ lived in an urban setting.

2. One of the founders of the Chartist Movement was _____ .

3. The now famous *Essay on the Principle of Population* first appearing in 1798 was written by _____ .

4. The earliest of the utopian socialists was _____ .

5. The socialist experiment at New Harmony, Indiana (U.S.A.) was established by _____ .

6. Charles Fourier's discussion of _____ was an early indication of a problem still confronting modern economic life.

7. Though the son of a middle-class factory owner, _____ was a close friend and fellow revolutionary of Karl Marx.

8. For _____ the fate of the working class would determine the fate of everyone else (i.e. the entire human race).

9. King Charles Albert of _____ led an early effort to rid northern Italy of Austrian domination.

10. The Frankfurt Parliament made little headway on the issue of German _____ .

11. The painting of the Great Western Railway in 1844 by _____ celebrated the industrial technology of the day in romantic style—using light and color more than line.

For Further Consideration

1. List three characteristics of early nineteenth-century industrialism, and relate them to a specific country if you can. What do the authors mean by saying that "industrialism grew on itself"?

2. How did industrialism change the working-class family in the first half of the nineteenth century?

3. Compare and contrast the utopian socialist ideas of Saint-Simon, Owen, and Fourier.

4. Define Marxism. Realistically, what were Marx's goals within the framework of his idea of the proletarian revolution?

or

Describe how Marx and Engels saw the movement of history, especially in the *Communist Manifesto*. From your own studies and other experience, what do you see as causes of history's movement?

5. Briefly review the revolutionary events of 1848 in France, Italy, Austria, and Germany. How is it that Russia and Great Britain were untouched by the contagion of revolution in this period? After achieving some initial successes, most of the revolutionary movements of 1848 failed. Why?

Answers

Multiple-Choice

Text page

1. B 417
2. A 414
3. B 416
4. A 416-417
5. D 418-419
6. B 418-419
7. B 423
8. A 426
9. D 426
10. A 428
11. A 424

True/False

1. F 413
2. T 414
3. T 416-417
4. T 417
5. F 419
6. T 419
7. T 420
8. F 422-423
9. T 425
10. F 426
11. T 422
12. T 418

Completion

1. England/Wales 413
2. William Lovett 416
3. Thomas Malthus 421
4. Count Saint-Simon .422
5. Robert Owen 422
6. boredom 422
7. Friedrich Engels 423
8. Karl Marx 424
9. Piedmont 428
10. unification 428
11. Joseph Maylord William Turner 415

23

The Age of Nation-States

Commentary

This chapter tells the story of the unification of Italy and of Germany, the reforms in the Hapsburg Empire, the restoration of republican government in France, and the continued development of Great Britain toward democracy.

The Crimean War (1854-1856) shattered the image of an invincible Russia, but more importantly it ended the Concert of Europe. The Concert of Europe was an informal agreement between nations to consult each other on foreign policy and to act together to maintain the balance of power set by the Congress of Vienna. For example, the Concert tried to lower the pressure of Napoleon III to redraw the European map to favor nationalities. The Concert also managed the opposite pressures of Austria and Prussia to increase their own power over the German Confederation. For about twenty-five years, instability prevailed in European affairs, and foreign policy increasingly became an instrument of domestic policy.

Nationalists had long wanted a unified Italian state, but had differed about the manner and goals of unification. Romantic republicans led by Mazzini and Garibaldi frightened more moderate Italians who looked instead to the Pope. Unification was carried out by Cavour, the almost conservative Prime Minister of Piedmont. Cavour attempted to prove to the rest of Europe that the Italians were capable of progressive government and that they were a military power. Cavour brought Piedmont into the Crimean War to make the latter point and played up to Napoleon III to gain his sympathy. The text goes on to detail the process of unification under Cavour's direction, including his thwarting the nationalist Guiseppe Garibaldi's vision for a republican Italy rather than a monarchy. In late 1860, Italy was united. Venetia was gained in 1866 and Rome was annexed in 1870. The Vatican retained its independence and remained hostile to the Italian state until 1929 when the state and papacy negotiated the Lateran Accord. As the newly united nation developed after 1870, its constitution provided for a rather conservative constitutional monarchy where Parliament had little power and much corruption.

The construction of a united German nation was the single most important political development in Europe between 1848 and 1914. It transformed the balance of economic, military and international power. Moreover, the character of the united German state was largely determined by its method of creation. Germany was united by a conservative army, monarchy (William I) and prime minister of Prussia (Bismarck), among whose chief motives was the outflanking of Prussian liberals. The text goes on to detail the process of unification through war, diplomacy and political manipulation.

The emergence of the two new unified states revealed the weakness of both France and the Hapsburg Empire. In 1870 Napoleon III was captured at the Battle of Sedan in September 1870. When the news reached Paris the French government repudiated Napoleon's monarchy and proclaimed a republic. Prussia besieged Paris until the city surrendered in January 1871. The new French National Assembly, elected in February, accepted Prussia's terms for peace. Terms included the Prussian occupation of France until the French paid a large indemnity. France also ceded Alsace and part of Lorraine to Prussia. Napoleon III was exiled.

Parisians had suffered under the Prussian siege and occupation of their city. Masses of residents, with a leadership including Jacobins and workers, broke with the French government and declared Paris a separate government from the rest of the country on March 28, 1871. The National Assembly ordered Paris bombarded in May. On May 21, the same day as the Assembly signed its treaty with Prussia, the Assembly's troops broke the Commune's defenses. About 20,000 Parisians were killed in the fight and bloody suppression occured afterwards—death on a scale comparable to the 25,000 people sacrificed in the Reign of Terror of the French Revolution. Monarchists failed in a bid to bring a king to the throne again. Instead, by 1875 the Third Republic had stabilized its authority in a President elected by universal male suffrage and in a two-chamber legislature. The Third Republic proved durable, surviving intrigues and scandals, such as bribes paid to politicians by a company constructing the Panama Canal. It also survived the infamous Dreyfus case.

In this case, Captain Alfred Dreyfus was found guilty in 1894 of passing information to the German army and sent to the notorious Devil's Island. Two years later, evidence surfaced that earlier evidence against Dreyfus had been forged. But Dreyfus was Jewish and French anti-Semitism reared up in the army, in the Catholic church, in conservative politicians and in some newspapers who insisted he was guilty. Then novelist Emile Zola countered the persecution with an article *J'accuse* (I Accuse), saying that the army was denying Dreyfus due process. Zola himself was convicted of libel, sentenced to prison, and forced to flee France for England. The political left—liberals, radicals and socialists—took up Dreyfus' cause. After dramatic twists and turns, including new military trials, a military suicide, a Presidential pardon and a civilian trial, Dreyfus was released. The left solidified its alliances and the conservatives similarly drew closer together, and the political repercussions of Dreyfus continued to divide the Third Republic until France's defeat by Germany early in World War II in 1940.

Austrian military defeats forced Francis Joseph to come to terms with the Magyar nobility of Hungary. through the Compromise of 1867, the Hapsburg Empire became a dual monarchy. Except for the common monarch, Austria and Hungary operated almost as separate states. Many of the other national groups within the empire opposed the Compromise of 1867 and political competition among various nationalist groups resulted in obstruction and a paralysis of parliamentary life.

Russia's defeat in the Crimean War compelled Alexander to make liberal reforms domestically. He abolished serfdom in 1861 officially, but th e government gave the serfs no land, instead reimbursing the serfs' former landlords for their losses. The government required the serfs to buy their land with unfavorable debt arrangements. The abolition of serfdom created the need for changes in local government and the judicial system, and Alexander introduced western-style reforms, such as trial by jury. But under the tsar, local government councils (zemstvos) received inadequate funds, and the tsar kept the power to override the court decisions by a judge and generally allowed no reforms that limited his own autocracy. Alexander II remained unpopular. After one attempt on his life in 1866, the tsar turned to repression and a police state. He was assassinated in 1881. Alexander III dedicated his reign to rolling back his father's reforms. His own son Nicholas II continued the reactionary polices that would contribute to the revolution of 1917.

While the continental nations became unified and struggled toward internal political restructuring, Great Britain continued to symbolize the confident liberal state. The Reform Act of 1867, passed by the Conservatives under the leadership of Disraeli, expanded the electorate well beyond the limits earlier proposed by the Liberals. In the long run, this secured a great deal of support for the Conservative party, but the immediate result was Gladstone's election as Prime Minister. Gladstone's ministry of 1868-1874 witnessed the culmination of British liberalism. It saw, among other things, passage of the Education Act of 1870, which created the first national system of schools. After a period of

Conservative leadership, Gladstone returned to office in 1880. The major issue of the next decade was Ireland. The Irish leader, who worked for a just land settlement and for home rule, was Charles Stewart Parnell. The Irish question remained unsolved until 1914 and affected British politics like the Austrian nationalities problem: a national domestic issue could not be adequately addressed because of political divisions.

Identifications

Identify each one of the following as used in the text. Refer to the text as necessary.

	Text page
romantic republicanism	432
Concert of Europe	432
Italia Irredenta	435
Count Vincent Benedetti	436-438
Battle of Sedan	438
Treaty of Frankfurt	439
Paris Commune	439
Marshal MacMahon	439
George Boulanger	439
"*J'accuse*/I accuse"	440
"neoabsolutism"	441
Edouard Manet and Impressionism	441
October Diploma	442
Russian Emancipation Proclamation	444
Alexander Herzen	445
Vera Zasulich	445
People's Will	445
Reform Act of 1867	446
Public Health Act/Artisans Dwelling Act of 1875	447-448
Irish Land League	448
Home Rule Bill	448

Map Exercise A

On this map of Italy, locate each of the following areas and cities.

Kingdom of the Two Sicilys	Brescia
Piedmont	Turin
Lombardy	Milan
Papal States	Palermo
Corsica	Naples
Sardinia	

Do your own research, using maps from throughout the text and also see page vi of this guide for additional references.

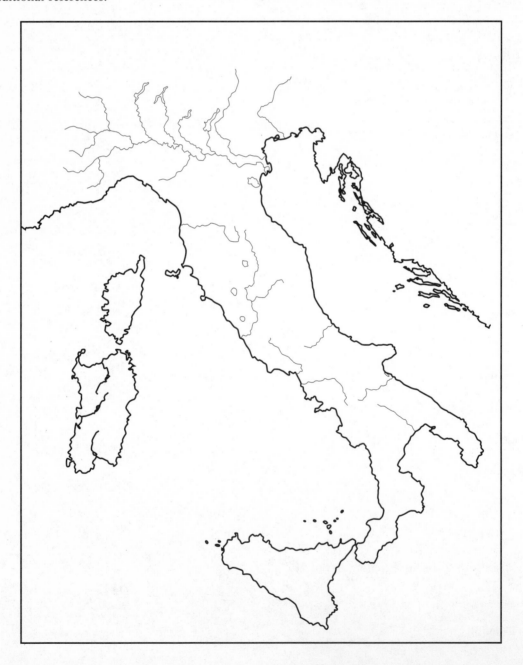

Map Exercise B

On this map of Germany, locate each of the following areas and cities.

Jutland Peninsula   Schleswig-Holstein
France   Alsace-Lorraine
Denmark   Belgium
Prussia   Munich
Bavaria   Berlin

Do your own research, using maps from throughout the text and also see page vi of this guide for additional references.

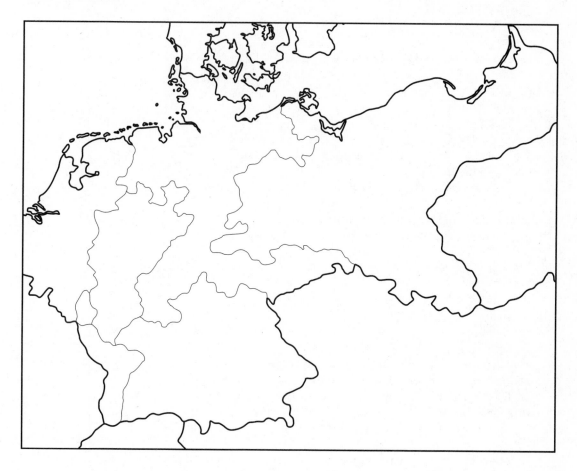

Short-Answer Exercises

Multiple-Choice

_____1. Which is the most accurate statement concerning the Crimean War?
   (a) both sides had well-equipped armies
   (b) after the war instability prevailed in Europe for several decades
   (c) the Concert of Europe ended
   (d) there was no formal peace treaty to end the war

_____2. The person most responsible for the final unification of Italy in 1861 was:
   (a) Niccolò Machiavelli
   (b) Guiseppe Garibaldi
   (c) Camillo Cavour
   (d) Felice Orsini

_____3. During the 1860s the Papal States were guarded by the troops of:
   (a) Piedmont
   (b) Austria
   (c) France
   (d) Prussia

_____4. Junker Otto von Bismarck's reactionary views disturbed even the arch-conservative German king but Bismarck:
   (a) made his mark as a politician and ambassador to Russia
   (b) allied with liberals favoring tax cuts
   (c) tried to avoid war, unless diplomacy failed
   (d) avoided political organizations, even as a university student

_____5. The immediate origins of the Franco-Prussian War lie in troubles within the monarchy of:
   (a) Prussia
   (b) France
   (c) Spain
   (d) Denmark

_____6. Napoleon III pursued his larger goals, in granting the legislature and press more freedoms and in lifting a ban on labor unions, to:
   (a) bolster support for government after losses in wars abroad
   (b) punish the army through an anti-war press
   (c) revitalize Paris, a union city, as the capital of liberal politics

_____7. A politician who acquired considerable prestige in France's turbulent politics of the 1880s and who might have led a successful coup against the Third Republic was:
   (a) Adolphe Thiers
   (b) George Boulanger
   (c) Marshal MacMahon
   (d) Leon Gambetta

_____8. Before the 1860s the usual period of service for Russian military recruits was:

(a) 6 months
(b) 5 years
(c) 10 years
(d) 25 years

_____9. The Russian monarch Alexander III:
(a) freed the serfs
(b) was a thoroughgoing reformer
(c) was the grandfather of Nicholas II
(d) was autocratic and reactionary

_____10. Two of the most important Prime Ministers of England during the 1860s and 1870s were:
(a) Peel and Derby
(b) Disraeli and Gladstone
(c) Palmerston and Aberdeen
(d) Cross and Russell

_____11. *Impressionism*, the late nineteenth-century style of painting that transformed the art of the Western world:
(a) painted to capture light
(b) often portrayed the leisure-time of city people of the middle or lower classes
(c) favored bright colors
(d) all of the above

True/False

_____1. The best known Romantic republican of this era was Victor Emmanuel III of Piedmont-Sardinia.

_____2. The papacy remained hostile to Italian unification into one state until the twentieth century.

_____3. When his brother Frederick William IV was judged insane, William I effectively became the ruler of Prussia.

_____4. Otto von Bismarck believed that German unification could be accomplished through Prussia's conservative constitution.

_____5. At the end of the Franco-Prussian War Louis Napoleon III was put on display in the Hall of Mirrors at Versailles Palace.

_____6. The Paris Commune quickly became a legend throughout Europe, including among Marxists who claimed it was a proletarian revolution suppressed by greedy aristocrats.

_____7. In 1871 the Bourbon claimant to the throne refused to accept the revolutionary flag of France and was therefore bypassed in favor of the formation of the Third French Republic.

_____8. Installed during the revolutions of 1848, the Hapsburg Emperor of Austria ruled for the next 58 years.

_____9. In the last quarter of the last century, territorial integrity became the single most important factor in defining a nation.

_____10. The Education Act of 1870 and the Ballot Act of 1872 grew out of British conservative politics which privatized education and limited voting to the educated.

_____11. The Folies-Bergere, around 1882, was Paris' leading music hall and was more like a popular music club with animal acts than it was a concert hall.

Completion

1. _____ was the one nation outside of Piedmont that was particularly supportive of the movement for Italian unification.

2. A function of mid-century Italian politics, the policy of _____ was rooted in bribery and corruption.

3. In the 1860s _____ led a French-supported expedition against Spanish rule in Mexico.

4. One of the most scandalous revelations of anti-Semitism and of military corruption in French life in the 1890s involved an army officer named _____ .

5. *J'accuse* was written by the French novelist _____ to protest an unjust trial.

6. _____ was the agreement between the Austrian emperor and Hungarian Magyars which gave Hungary nominal self-rule in the so-called Dual Monarchy.

7. The Russian nobility tried to play a large role in the local government's councils called _____, but faced underfunded provincial budgets.

8. A revolutionary movement based around peasants and supported by many students, intellectuals, and radicals in Russia was known as _____ .

9. The _____ Party of Britain worked generally to block Irish Home Rule in the late nineteenth century.

10. The leader of the movement for Irish Home Rule was _____ .

For Further Consideration

1. Sum up as briefly as you can the main motives of the Russian and Ottoman Empire and of the other participants in the Crimean War. What were at least two effects of the war?

2. Compare and contrast the processes involved in the unification of Italy with those involved in the unification of Germany.

3. What led absolutism to backfire in The Hapsburg (Austria-Hungary) Empire under Francis Joseph?

4. Sum up the main reasons for Britain's reputation as a model of a stable, liberal state among the European governments of the nineteenth century.

5. Looking at Russia in the last half of the nineteenth-century, point out at least three of the most strik-ing signs of why tsarist rule was called "reactionary." Then describe any aspect of the opposing revolu-tionary movement of young Russians. What, if anything, does the conflict remind you of today?

6. Describe the main features of nationalism of the last 25 years of the nineteenth century. Use at least one country or people to illustrate. What reminds you of this today? Or, what has changed?

Answers

Multiple-Choice

		Text page
1.	C	432
2.	C	432
3.	C	435
4.	A	436-437
5.	C	438
6.	A	438
7.	B	439
8.	D	445
9.	D	445-446
10.	B	446-447
11.	D	441

True/False

1.	F	432-433
2.	T	435
3.	T	436
4.	T	438
5.	F	438
6.	F	439
7.	T	439
8.	F	440
9.	F	443
10.	F	447
11.	T	441

Completion

1.	France	433
2.	*transformismo*	435
3.	Archduke Maximilian of Austria	438
4.	Alfred Dreyfus	439-440
5.	Emile Zola	439-440
6.	*Ausgleich*/Compromise of 1867	443
7.	*zemstvos*	445
8.	Populism	445
9.	Conservative (Tory)	448
10.	Charles Stewart Parnell	448

24

The Building of European Supremacy:
Society and Politics to World War I

Commentary

The half-century before the outbreak of World War I (1914–1918) clearly established the foundations upon which much of Western civilization now rests. The related growth of population, capitalism, industry, and urban centers was rapidly changing the European landscape and outlook by the last half of the nineteenth century. A significantly advanced phase of industrial development was for a second time revolutionizing the European world. Electricity, higher-grade steel, and petrochemicals spurred new industries based upon resources and technologies that were more than mere forerunners of today's industrial maturity. Large corporations, cartels, and multinational business interests were transferring the older economic principles into our own modern concepts. These facts alone caused a widespread reappraisal of social, economic, and political life.

Governments and their industrial powers were more ready than ever to serve each other's mutual needs. A new social consciousness emerged and was coupled directly with the growth of an ambitious and energetic middle class. The roles of women and children within this rising class set a pattern not changed until our own time, and still not entirely changed. For example, recent research better explains the expectations and roles of working and middle-class women. Equally interesting is how current studies of prostitution in this era counter some of the myths associated with this occupation. Although the position of the working classes was still inferior, many workers now enjoyed a way of life and a standard of living that easily eclipsed that of the previous half-century. Notable among these benefits were the efforts in city planning and reconstruction that were designed to advance the nation's commercial interests and enhance the living environs of the various social classes. There were additional indications that the economic growth and related benefits would continue for all classes of people.

Naturally these events were not without their tensions. Socialism moved from the pens of the theorists of the pre–1848 era to a position of acceptability and respectability throughout much of Europe. At the same time the many versions of socialism were constantly debated throughout the times, and their many and wide-ranging interpretations prevented the socialists from achieving a united front. This pattern, however, differed in each nation of Europe. In Britain, where political compromise and accommodation were an already accepted and popular mode of resolving conflict, Parliament sought change that at least moderately incorporated the ideas of the reformers.

On the continent less compromise can be seen. "Opportunism" in France received little acceptance. The French picture was further clouded by the Dreyfus Affair at the end of the century. In Germany, Bismarckian political maneuvers managed to keep the Social Democrats off guard until after 1900. Their socialist reform programs were often eclipsed by the overall growth and economic successes of that nation.

By the end of the century Russian socialism had emerged as the most radical continental movement. With Russia's late entrance into industrialization and agricultural reform, a situation exacerbated by the success evidenced in other nations, that country's progress was almost stillborn. Conservative-minded czars managed to stay in power by cultivating the nobility, controlling the relatively small commercial classes, and sometimes ruthlessly quelling worker unrest—as in the Revolution of 1905.

On the eve of World War I, which came on the heels of dramatic economic growth in Europe, socialist reform programs can be viewed as a mixture of successes and failures. But their programs and efforts, though temporarily stemmed by the war, were to be a permanent part of the Western heritage.

Identifications

Identify each one of the following as used in the text. Refer to the text as necessary.

Map Exercise A

On the accompanying map locate each of the capital cities of Europe:

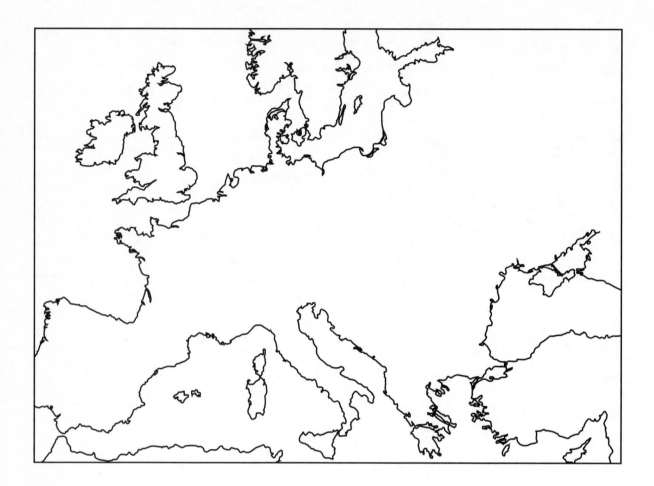

Map Exercise B

On the accompanying map of Western Russia, show each of the following.

Gulf of Finland   Moscow
Lake Ladoga   Germany
St. Petersburg   Austria-Hungary
Baltic Sea   Dnieper River
Finland   Volga River

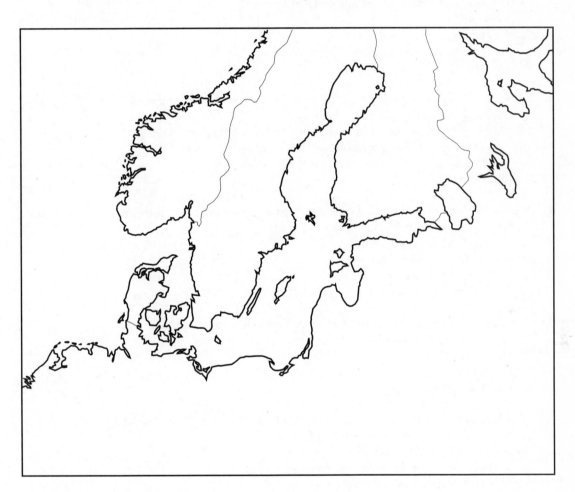

Short-Answer Exercises

Multiple-Choice

_____1.   Between 1860 and 1914:
(a) Europe's financial and industrial supremacy emerged
(b) socialism became an influential part of European political life
(c) the modern basis of the welfare state emerged in Europe
(d) all of these occurred

_____2.   By 1910 the population of Europe reached nearly:
(a) 600 million
(b) 450 million
(c) 300 million
(d) 150 million.

_____3.   Which of the following is an accurate statement about the development of European cities in the second half of the nineteenth century?
(a) the central portions of many major cities were redesigned
(b) residents began to look for housing outside of city centers
(c) commercialization of city centers took place
(d) all of these

_____4.   Important new medical practices became a part of European life in this era because of the research of all of the following, except:
(a) Georges Haussmann in France
(b) Robert Koch in Germany
(c) Joseph Lister in Britain
(d) Louis Pasteur in France

_____5.   The most advanced women's movement in Europe could be found in:
(a) Austro-Hungarian Empire
(b) Great Britain
(c) France
(d) the Netherlands

_____6.   Which of the following is the most correct statement about trades unions by 1900?
(a) they were completely suppressed in Germany
(b) most members were unskilled laborers
(c) they were legalized in Germany, England, and France
(d) only Great Britain permitted their existence

_____7.   The collapse of the First International is least attributed to:
(a) the success of British unionism
(b) the growth and influence of other socialist organizations
(c) events surrounding the Paris Commune
(d) moving its headquarters to the United States

_____8. Type of socialism that aimed at gradual and peaceful change within the existing social-political framework was known as:
  (a) trade unionism
  (b) Marxism
  (c) Fabianism
  (d) syndicalism

_____9. Bismarck's response to the efforts of the German socialists was:
  (a) a repression of the socialist parties
  (b) health insurance
  (c) government-sponsored social welfare programs
  (d) all of these

_____10. Known as Lenin, the most notable Russian Marxist of the nineteenth century:
  (a) Vladimir Ulyanov
  (b) Gregory Plekhanov
  (c) Sergei Witte
  (d) P. A. Stolypin

True/False

_____1. The out-migration of Europeans to the United States, Canada, South Africa, and Argentina had the effect of relieving social pressures on the Continent.

_____2. Concern for urban riots was among the factors which prompted Louis Napoleon's rebuilding of the city of Paris.

_____3. In the last half of the nineteenth century it became clear that new urban water and sewer systems would achieve considerable health benefits for the entire population.

_____4. Among the female population at this time, women who did not marry probably had the best time of it.

_____5. Continuous demonstrations by the "suffragettes" brought British women the franchise in 1918.

_____6. Pogroms protected Jews from violence in Russia.

_____7. The membership of the First International included Polish nationalists, socialists, political radicals, and even anarchists.

_____8. For participating in a plot against Tzar Alexander III, Lenin's older brother was executed in 1887.

_____9. "Bloody Sunday" was a 1905 event in which several thousand Russian workers and poor successfully attacked the Tzar's Winter Palace in Saint Petersburg.

_____10. The authors of the text assert that during the latter part of the nineteenth century Europe experienced the emergence of socialism, labor unions, contradictory lifestyles, and growing demands of women in politics.

Completion

1. The growth of the chemical industry at the end of the nineteenth century was especially fostered by this nation: _____ .

2. The single most important aspect of the later industrial revolution was in the use of _____ for production.

3. After 1850 the _____ became the arbiter of consumer taste and defender of the status quo.

4. The _____ was a monument to the material comforts that industrialization provided for middle-class life.

5. _____ was a word used to depict instances of cooperation between French socialists and the government.

6. _____ was the author of *Evolutionary Socialism* (1899).

7. The person who led Russia into the industrial age was _____ .

8. In Russia the more prosperous peasant farmers were known as _____ .

9. Lenin's group within the Russian Social Democratic Party was known as the _____ .

10. Instrumental in causing serious unrest in Russia in 1905 was that country's defeat by _____ .

For Further Consideration

1. Explain in detail the differences between the First and Second Industrial Revolutions.

2. Describe the position of women within the middle-class household and within society generally at the end of the nineteenth century.

3. Describe in detail the key elements of the feminist movement at the end of the nineteenth and into the early part of the twentieth century. Be sure to discuss the leading personalities of the movement and list their most important goals.

4. Compare and contrast any three of the non-Russian socialist theories of this era.

5. As exemplified in his pamphlet *What Is to Be Done?* what were Lenin's ideas and how were they different from the ideas of those in the Russian Social Democratic party?

Answers

Multiple-Choice

		Text page
1.	D	450-451
2.	B	451
3.	D	454
4.	A	455
5.	B	460
6.	C	462
7.	D	462-463
8.	C	463
9.	D	466
10.	A	467

True/False

1.	T	451
2.	T	454
3.	T	455
4.	F	455-458
5.	T	458
6.	F	461
7.	T	462-463
8.	T	467
9.	T	468
10.	F	469

Completion

1.	Germany	452
2.	electricity	452
3.	middle class	453
4.	London Great Exhibition of 1851	453
5.	Opportunism	466
6.	Eduard Bernstein	466
7.	Sergei Witte	467
8.	*kulaks*	467
9.	Bolsheviks	468
10.	Japan	468

25

The Birth of Modern European Thought

Commentary

Any adequate understanding of the world we live in today requires serious consideration and thorough understanding of those strains of thought associated with the turn of the nineteenth century. The changes that occurred in scientific and intellectual thinking and outlook during Europe's Victorian era should not be underestimated.

These changes were stimulated by an increasingly literate and better-educated public. The increase in education, coupled with wider and cheaper means of printing and distribution, brought men and women all over Europe in touch with the scientific and intellectual community as never before. This contact, however, was also to introduce the general public mind to many iconoclastic viewpoints that further increased the social and political tensions of the era.

As in a previous period of Western history, it was science that initially stimulated new outlooks. The mechanistic principles of nature established during the Enlightenment underwent considerable transformation. Theories of evolution, related racial theories, modern atomic principles, and Freudian psychology, combined with an ever-increasing view of the ability of science to solve all humankind's problems, shattered many ideas long accepted. The organized churches of Europe were assaulted from several sides and placed on the defensive as never before. Christianity now found itself in opposition to much of what was happening. Many governments, inspired by religion's defensive posture, made inroads on a number of previously accepted areas of church authority. In Germany this assault was highlighted by Bismarck's *Kulturkampf*. The most powerful religious organization, the Roman Catholic Church, under Popes Pius IX and Leo XIII, had exceptional difficulties in adapting to the new scientific and intellectual positions. Yet by the end of the era most church organizations remained as viable parts of Europe's social, political, and cultural life.

This era is notable for the widespread social criticism that was stimulated by the scientific ferment and enunciated by articulate writers. A new "realism" in literature, which criticized almost all romantic notions, left no stone unturned in examining the less savory areas of human endeavor in the industrial age. Poverty, prostitution, and the bourgeois family with its hapless female adjuncts were all subjects for critical examination.

Not only were society, industrial life, and culture attacked, but with Nietzsche and other irrationalist writers the whole basis of the new criticism itself, reason, was challenged. For Nietzsche the philosophical assumptions of all Western civilization were wrong and in serious need of re-evaluation. The birth of contemporary European thought is clearly seen with the advent of Freud's teachings. As Marx had previously caused a re-examination of the capitalist system and Darwin fostered a reassessment of major biological assumptions, Freud forced a serious look at the role of the subconscious. These three seminal thinkers, interpreting the new dimensions of human life, ushered in the world as we know it.

It is also clear today that the Feminist movement which emerged after World War II had roots in the modernist literary atmosphere of the late nineteenth century. Overshadowed by the events of two world wars, the contemporary movement, although still defining itself, is another sign of the rich intellectual heritage of the pre-World War I era.

During this era men and women challenged many of the underlying assumptions upon which Western thought was founded. Their works, despite frequent criticism and constant re-evaluation, remain basic to any competent understanding of the Western heritage today.

Identifications

Identify each one of the following as used in the text. Refer to the text as necessary.

	text page
Auguste Comte	472-473
Gregor Mendel	473
"ethical imperative" of Herbert Spencer	474
Ernst Mach and Henri Poincaré	477
Wilhelm Roentgen	477
"uncertainty principle"	478
Henrik Ibsen	478
Igor Stravinsky	479
Bloomsbury Group	479
Thus Spoke Zarathrustra	479
id, ego, and superego	482
Max Weber	482-483
Georges Sorel	483
Aryans	483
Houston Stewart Chamberlain	483
Karl Lueger	484
Theodor Herzl	484
Contagious Diseases Act	485

Map Exercise

On the map following this list place the boundaries and names of the European countries; within those boundaries place the number for the name of the person listed. You should use the country of birth; but in some cases the place of work should be noted. You may need to consult other sources.

1. Joseph Breuer
2. Houston S. Chamberlain
3. Auguste Comte
4. Marie and Pierre Curie
5. Charles Darwin
6. Sigmund Freud
7. Arthur de Gobineau
8. Thomas Henry Huxley

9. Henrik Ibsen
10. Carl Jung
11. Ellen Key
12. Julius Langbehn
13. Gustave LeBon
14. Karl Lueger
15. Thomas Mann
16. Karl Marx

17. Gregor Mendel
18. Friedrich Nietzsche
19. Pope Leo XIII
20. J.J. Thomson
21. Max Weber
22. Julius Wellhausen
23. Virginia Woolf

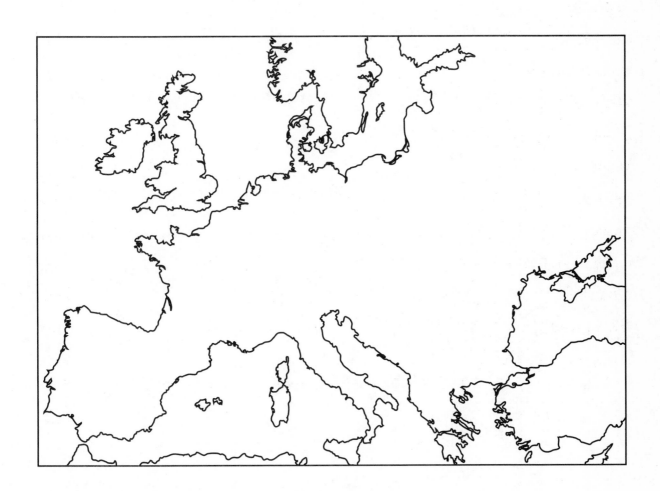

Short-Answer Exercises

Multiple-Choice

_____1. By the turn of the century which of the following European states had the highest literacy rate?
(a) Spain
(b) Austria-Hungary
(c) Belgium
(d) Italy

_____2. Three stages of human development—theological, metaphysical, and positivist—stem from the thought of:
(a) Émile Durkheim
(b) Auguste Comte
(c) Thomas Henry Huxley
(d) Claude Bernard

_____3. _____ in his *Life of Jesus* cast doubt on the origins of Christianity.
(a) Julius Wellhausen
(b) David Friederich Strauss
(c) William Robertson Smith
(d) Ernst Renan

_____4. The dogma of the infallibility of the pope in matters of faith and morals stems from the:
(a) concept of Catholic Modernism
(b) First Vatican Council
(c) *Rerum Novarum*
(d) *Syllabus of Errors*

_____5. Pope Leo XIII's encyclical *Rerum Novarum* supported all of the following except:
(a) just wages
(b) private property
(c) socialism
(d) religious education

_____6. _____ is considered to have discovered radium.
(a) Marie Curie
(b) Werner Heisenberg
(c) Anthony Brescia
(d) Max Planck

_____7. The word "overman" is most clearly associated with the thinking of:
(a) Friedrich Nietzsche
(b) Pope Pius XI
(c) George Gissing
(d) Émile Zola

_____8. "The dream is a fulfillment of a wish" would be a phrase best associated with:
(a) Friedrich Nietzsche
(b) Max Planck
(c) Sigmund Freud
(d) Leo Tolstoy

_____9. Which of the following names would not be considered as that of an anti-Semitic writer or politician?
(a) Theodor Herzl
(b) Adolf Stoecker
(c) Karl Lueger
(d) Houston S. Chamberlain

_____10. With *A Room of One's Own* Virginia Woolf opened:
(a) a new discussion of sexual morality
(b) the whole question of gender definition
(c) an assault against the male-dominated literary world
(d) demands for living space for single women

True/False

_____1. Intellectual life in the last half of the nineteenth century was altered by the existence of a mass reading audience.

_____2. In 1830 Charles Lyell established the basis of the modern theory of chemical composition.

_____3. The replacement of the Falloux Law of 1850 with the so-called Ferry Laws effectively removed religious education from the public schools of France.

_____4. At the turn of the century both Max Planck and Albert Einstein were challenging the conventional theories of physics.

_____5. In his *Androcles and the Lion* George Bernard Shaw praised Christianity's role throughout the ages.

_____6. Friedrich Nietzsche, whose first important philosophical work was titled *The Birth of Tragedy,* was actually trained in the study of ancient literary texts.

_____7. The Austrian physician Sigmund Freud believed that the innocence of childhood, particularly in regard to sexual things, should be preserved with great care until at least puberty.

_____8. The publication of Carl Jung's *Modern Man in Search of a Soul* in 1933 completely reversed Freud's views on dreams.

_____9. Arthur de Gobineau's theories of racial determinism expressed in his *Essay on the Inequality of the Human Races* noted that the process of degeneration would end within a century.

_____10. The idea that the Jews should establish their own nation (Zionism) is associated with the work of Theodor Herzl.

Completion

1. _____ was the scientist who first began to unravel the mystery of heredity.

2. The terms "evolutionary ethics" and "social Darwinism" are associated with the works of _____.

3. _____, a German philosopher, described Christianity as a religion for sheep—a glorification of weakness instead of the vigor of a full-blooded human life.

4. Pope Pius IX's issuance of the _____ was a clear sign of the Church's antiliberal stance.

5. _____ is often considered the first genuinely realistic novel.

6. In the play _____ George Bernard Shaw explored the matter of prostitution.

7. _____ wrote *To the Lighthouse*.

8. _____ was a student of Freud who later could not accept the idea that sex played the prime role in the formation of the human personality.

9. *The Protestant Ethic and the Spirit of Capitalism* was written by _____ .

10. Late in the nineteenth century _____ attitudes were fostered through a variety of factors such as pressures created by change, the insecurities of the new middle classes, and Jewish domination of money and banking interests.

For Further Consideration

1. Discuss several factors that gave rise to increased literacy in Europe by the end of the nineteenth century. Why was the increase in literacy so important to the intellectual and scientific developments of the era?

2. Examine the broad-based attacks upon the Christian churches in the late nineteenth century. What were the origins of these challenges to religious authority? What were the results?

3. Describe the views of the German writer Friedrich Nietzsche. Are his views relevant or irrelevant today?

4. How do you assess the impact of the works of Sigmund Freud? What were the chief positions taken in his pioneering studies?

5. Discuss the foundations of the Feminist movement at the turn of the century. Why was there an insistence upon defining gender roles?

Answers

Multiple-Choice

		Text page
1.	C	472
2.	B	472
3.	B	474
4.	B	476
5.	C	476
6.	A	477
7.	A	481
8.	C	482
9.	A	483-484
10.	B	486

True/False

1.	T	472
2.	F	474
3.	T	475
4.	T	477
5.	F	478
6.	T	479
7.	F	482
8.	F	482
9.	F	483
10.	T	484

Completion

1.	Gregor Mendel	473
2.	Herbert Spencer	474
3.	Friedrich Nietzsche	475
4.	*Syllabus of Errors*	476
5.	*Madame Bovary*	478
6.	*Mrs. Warren's Profession*	478
7.	Virginia Woolf	479
8.	Carl Jung	482
9.	Max Weber	483
10.	anti-Semitic	484

26

Imperialism, Alliances, and War

Commentary

The economic and technological advances made within the European system virtually Europeanized the world by the end of the nineteenth century. Never before had one section of the globe held such far-reaching authority over another. And the situation was evident to peoples at both ends of this "new Imperialism." The process of modern European development, normally associated with the Renaissance, the Scientific Revolution, and the Enlightenment, had resulted in the demonstrable European superiority. From their superior position the great powers of Europe, and somewhat belatedly Japan, were able to reach out and establish colonial control over less-developed, nonindustrial areas. This colonializing process was most evident on the African continent; there, competition between the European states was a factor that drove on the explorers, missionaries, traders, bankers, and politicians. The conditions of this "new Imperialism," unlike those of earlier periods of international competition, engaged all sectors of a nation's social, economic, and political life. This engagement intensified the already stimulated sense of nationalism felt in Europe. As a result, by 1900 the European states were practically realigned into a bipolar alliance system. And, in retrospect, there were clear signs—Italy and France in North Africa; Austria and Russia in the Balkans; France and England in Central Africa; Germany and England in East Africa; Japan, China, and Russia in Asia—that imperialist concerns could lead to steadily increasing serious confrontations.

Recognizing these factors, the great powers looked to their armies and navies as more necessary than ever before. Consequently militarism, as a condition of life, became a norm. The acceleration of technological development greatly increased military needs, expenditures, and training programs as the developing alliance system demanded larger armed forces. Imperial concerns, coupled with increased rivalries between the great powers, called forth the new alliance system in Europe inaugurated by the Austro-German (Dual) Alliance of 1879.

The smashing success of Germany in defeating France and establishing the German Empire changed the nature of European power politics. The unification of Germany, unlike that of Italy, was a success virtually from the start. The weaknesses often associated with newly formed states were not apparent in the new German Empire. The defeat of France and the establishment of the German Empire set in motion a chain of events not entirely concluded even today. The destiny of France was immediately tied to avenging this "humiliation" by Germany. For the satisfied German government, under the masterful influence of Bismarck, the future lay in maintaining the status quo, developing to Germany's benefit the enormous gains that were a part of the French defeat and the German unification. In less than a decade, however, the European states were moved into an ever-widening consideration of rivalries as a result of their extension into Africa and Asia. For the Austro-Hungarian Empire and the Russian Empire, this expansive mood brought conflicts closer to home in the crumbling European empire of the Ottoman Turks—the Balkans. Here an infectious nationalism that was centered in Serbia and Bulgaria caused growing unrest. The Russian intervention there that led to the 1878 Congress of Berlin was a forerunner of future problems. By the 1890s Germany, Austria-Hungary, and Italy had formed the Triple Alliance, and France and Russia had been drawn together in a mutual defense pact. In 1902 Britain left behind her "splendid isolation" to form an alliance with Japan. Then she was drawn into the Franco-Russian orbit, forming the *Entente Cordiale* with France in 1904 and a similar agreement with Russia in 1907.

Though imperial rivalries continued worldwide, the unresolved problem through the early 1900s was the Balkans. Conflicts between the Balkan nationalities themselves, the weakness of the Ottoman Empire, and the conflicting ambitions of Russia and Austria left the area with an unclosable wound. In this context the assassination of the Austrian heir in June 1914 at Sarajevo proved catastrophic. The chain of events that followed, the competition, the fears, the misunderstandings of the previous half-century, quickly transformed the Balkan crisis into the immediate cause of World War I.

For 51 months the military of the European states slugged it out on battlefields and seas throughout the world. Before the war ended over 30 states were involved, including the United States, and the casualties totaled over 30 million. The European world, so safe, secure, and stable, had blown up. The task of repairing the damage of so great a conflict fell on the shoulders of mere mortals, who as heads of state had to follow their political instincts, their people's demands, and not always their consciences. The Peace of Paris, the Versailles settlement, was the product of long labor but was negotiated under such embittered conditions that the peacemakers' treaty became a problem even before it was completed. Too much had changed in such a short period of time, and errors were made that were destined to haunt future generations.

The decision not to include Germany in the Peace Conference was a fateful one because it left the door wide open to future uncertainty. It was similarly unwise to exclude the Soviet Union. To ignore so great a revolution as had occurred in Russia was at least shortsighted. The great Russian state had entered the war with mixed emotions, uncertain in direction, with a weakened military machine, with serious political and economic problems, and a populace no longer convinced of the tzar's authority. For that country to have sent its soldiers against the best army in Europe was itself a travesty. By 1917 revolutions in Russia had brought the Bolsheviks under Lenin to power. What would have seemed inconceivable three years before was a reality. Russia was to be transformed. Resistance to the Bolshevik takeover continued within Russia, taking the form of a civil war between "Red" Russians who supported the revolution and "White" Russians who opposed it. By 1921, however, the Bolsheviks had complete control of the state.

In the early 1920s the Bolsheviks busied themselves with securing what they envisioned to be the Soviet future. A process today is seemingly going on in reverse. The world once so clearly dominated by western Europe would soon experience the strains awakened by radical ideologies emerging at war's end. The Europeans themselves, so confident a generation before, faced new uncertainties that undermined what security remained in the aftermath of World War I.

Identifications

Identify each one of the following as used in the text; refer to the text as necessary.

	text page
"New Imperialism"	489
Treaty of San Stefano	492
The Triple Alliance	494
the Boer War	495
Entente Cordiale	495
Young Turks	496
Panther	497
London Conference of 1913	497
Conrad von Hötzendorf	498
Schlieffen Plan	499, 501
Erich Ludendorff	501
Erich von Falkenhayn	503
Lusitania	504
Leon Trotsky	505
Treaty of Brest-Litovsk	505
Fourteen Points	505
Philipp Scheidmann	509

Map Exercise A

Name/locate the major bodies of water surrounding the African continent.

Devise a color or shading scheme to show the areas of European colonial control throughout the African continent for each of the following states:

Great Britain	Italy
Germany	Spain
France	Portugal
Belgium	

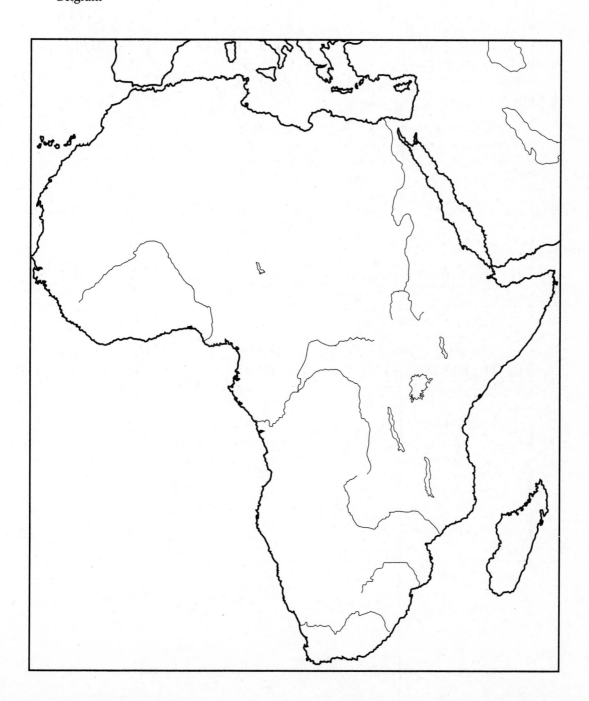

Map Exercise B

Mark the appropriate boundaries of those eastern European countries which appeared at the end of World War I.

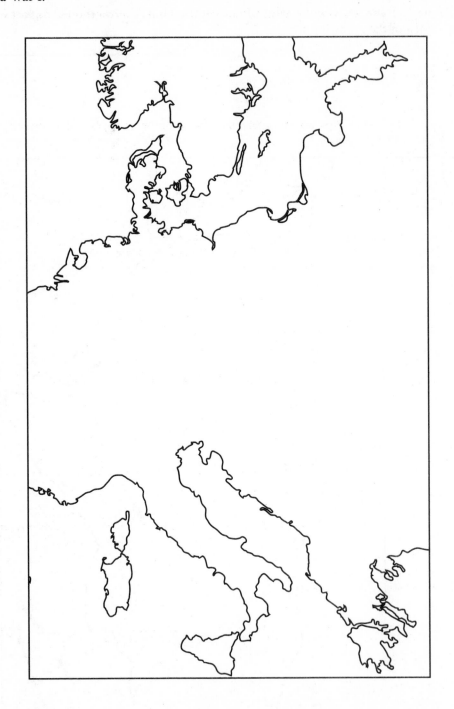

Short-Answer Exercises

Multiple-Choice

_____1. Which of the following countries did not seek to establish African colonies as part of the New Imperialism?
(a) Italy
(b) Russia
(c) Belgium
(d) Britain

_____2. Which of the following areas was the least vulnerable to European expansion at the end of the nineteenth century?
(a) China
(b) South America
(c) Ottoman Empire
(d) Africa

_____3. Which of the following is not a result of the Congress of Berlin of 1878?
(a) Austria-Hungary "gained" the provinces of Bosnia and Herzegovina
(b) Germany and Russia would soon drift further apart
(c) Bulgaria was reduced in size
(d) all of these were the results of the meeting

_____4. The three states of the Triple Alliance were:
(a) Germany, Russia, and Austria-Hungary
(b) Great Britain, France, and Russia
(c) Germany, Austria-Hungary, and Italy
(d) Russia, France, and Serbia

_____5. The three states of the Triple Entente were:
(a) Germany, Russia, and Austria-Hungary
(b) Great Britain, France, and Russia
(c) Germany, Austria-Hungary, and Italy
(d) Russia, France, and Serbia

_____6. Of all of the major powers involved, which of the two appear to have been most responsible for the outbreak of the World War I?
(a) Great Britain and France
(b) Germany and Great Britain
(c) Russia and Austria-Hungary
(d) Germany and Austria

_____7. Throughout the war the most effective basic new weapon was the:
(a) machine gun
(b) tank
(c) submarine
(d) airplane

_____8. Lenin and the Bolsheviks signed the Treaty of Brest-Litovsk in 1918 because:
(a) Russia was not able to carry on the war effort
(b) Lenin's government needed time to impose its will on the Russian people
(c) Lenin believed that communism would soon sweep through the warring states of Europe
(d) all of these

_____9. One of the factors that appeared to hasten the peacemakers at Paris to conclude the Treaty of Versailles was:
(a) the threat of a renewed war with Germany
(b) the near-collapse of France
(c) President Wilson's political problems at home
(d) none of these

_____10. With regard to eastern Europe the settlements of the Paris Peace Conference included all of the following except:
(a) Bulgaria was enlarged from territory of Greece and Yugoslavia
(b) the complete disappearance of the Austro-Hungarian Empire
(c) Finland, Estonia, Latvia, and Lithuania became independent states
(d) the Magyars were left in control of the new Hungarian state

True/False

_____1. A novel aspect of the so-called New Imperialism was the efforts of the imperial power to integrate the native inhabitants into the managerial structure of the colony.

_____2. During this period the English statesman Joseph Chamberlain advanced the idea of overseas empires serving as a source of profit that could be utilized to finance domestic reform and welfare programs in the home country.

_____3. The effort to keep France isolated in Europe was a cornerstone of Bismarck's policy.

_____4. The First Moroccan Crisis was temporarily resolved at an 1906 international meeting held at Portsmouth, New Hampshire (U.S.A.).

_____5. An integral part of the Second Moroccan Crisis was the British assumption that Germany was moving to establish a naval base there.

_____6. The assassination of Archduke Francis Ferdinand and his wife in Sarajevo was condemned everywhere in Europe.

_____7. At the time of the outbreak of World War I the mobilization of the armed forces of any country was interpreted as a bluff and not to be taken seriously.

_____8. Italy was lured into World War I against Germany and Austria-Hungary as a result of territorial promises made by the Western Allies.

_____9. Russian Mensheviks believed, like Karl Marx, that a proletarian revolution could occur only after the bourgeois stage of development.

_____10. At the end of World War I a right-wing group emerged under the name of "Spartacus" and challenged the newly established government of Germany.

Completion

1. As part of the New Imperialism, European nations employed new strategies, such as annexation, protectorate status, and the establishment of _____ in their attempts to assert direct control over foreign lands.

2. Although Germany declared protectorates over Namibia, _____, the Cameroons, and Tanzania, Bismarck had no interest in the African colonies for themselves; he hoped that African colonies could be used as bases to put pressure on Britain and to provide outlets for France's hostility.

3. The so-called _____ brought the empires of Germany, Russia, and Austria-Hungary together in 1873.

4. _____ was the country that gained the least from the 1878 Congress of Berlin.

5. Bismarck's successor, _____, was unable to maintain the delicate system of alliances created by Bismarck.

6. The architect of the new German navy was _____ .

7. It can be said that Britain's isolation ended with her treaty with _____ .

8. "They shall not pass" is a slogan associated with the great battle of _____ .

9. _____ and _____ were nations both excluded from the newly formed League of Nations.

10. The League of Nations had no armed forces of its own, but planned to enforce its edicts by _____ and by military interventions sponsored by its members.

For Further Consideration

1. Discuss several of the causes of the so-called "New Imperialism." In your opinion which countries in their colonial efforts gained an advantage and which countries gained little or nothing for their efforts?

2. Give an overall year-by-year review of the important military strategies and events of World War I.

3. Describe the economic and political realities in Russia during World War I. In your opinion should Lenin and the Bolsheviks have been surprised at their seemingly sudden success? Explain your answer fully.

4. In an analysis of the results of the Versailles settlement list what can be considered as specific successes and failures of the Paris Peace Conference of 1919? Briefly explain each one.

5. Compare and contrast the conditions of European politics and society that existed at the time of the Congress of Vienna (1815) with those existing at the time of the Paris Peace Conference (1919).

Answers

Multiple-Choice

		Text page
1.	B	.491
2.	B	.491-492
3.	D	.494
4.	C	.494
5.	B	.496
6.	C	.497
7.	A	.501
8.	D	.505
9.	B	.507
10.	A	.507, 509

True/False

1.	F	.489
2.	T	.490-491
3.	T	.492
4.	T	.496
5.	T	.497
6.	F	.498
7.	F	.499
8.	T	.501
9.	T	.504
10.	F	.507

Completion

1.	Spheres of influence	.489
2.	Togoland	.491
3.	Three Emporers' League	.492
4.	Russia	.494
5.	Leo von Caprivi	.495
6.	Alfred von Tirpitz	.495
7.	Japan	.495
8.	Verdun	.503
9.	Germany; Soviet Union	.507
10.	economic sanctions	.507

27
Political Experiments of the 1920s

Commentary

If the foundations of today's world were laid down in World War I, then the 1920s can be viewed as the time of attempting to build the first floor. The Peace of Paris, although intended to bring stability and trust to a war-weary Europe, turned out to be cement that never dried. Instead of security, each of the war's participants had complaints. Germany had been embarrassed, and the reparations demands led to endless disputes. The newly established eastern European states could not accept their newly created boundaries. As it turned out, the architects could not agree, causing demand for frequent renovations. So disturbed was the European world after the war that the efforts at stabilization and reorganization were often met with skepticism and outright violence. The political experiments of the 1920s were wide-ranging and drew upon ideas from many of the theorists of the prewar era. Yet never before had governments become so much a part of their citizens' lives. World War I had caused massive centralization and control within the belligerent countries, a process that was to continue in peacetime. Considerable shifts in the sociological landscape also followed in the wake of war. Each country looked to a variety of approaches in an attempt to combine pre-war ideas with the new forces generated by the war. The successes and failures of this postwar decade, like those of other historic eras, were affected by the leaders who shaped the new social, economic, and political world. Accompanying the postwar European financial, and its related social, unrest was the reality of the growing international competition from the United States and Japan.

Russia, as we have seen, had not even made it through the war. In 1917 a series of uprisings led to the Bolshevik success at the end of the year. In the following years, Lenin and his successors ruthlessly installed a wholly new socialist and totalitarian order. Though initially challenged by many groups, the Bolsheviks, aided by Leon Trotsky's genius, won out. By 1921 Lenin's New Economic Policy (NEP) promised to restore economic stability to Russia. With Lenin's death and the subsequent power struggle that followed, Josef Stalin was eventually able to establish his own permanent dictatorship. Despite the massive brutality involved, Stalin inaugurated a system that came to dominate Soviet political and economic thought into the last quarter of this century. As you will read in Chapter 30, the system built by Stalin since the late 1920s would be installed throughout eastern Europe at the end of World War II. Ultimately, "Stalinism" remains a phrase associated with extremely repressive dictators and unfortunately, in that sense, continues to affect world consciousness.

In Italy the 1920s took a different turn. Though on the victorious side, Italy was angered by the terms of the Versailles agreements because Italian territorial ambitions were thwarted. This factor, coupled with the severe internal disruptions caused by the war, brought the collapse of the parliamentary system there in 1922. In that year Benito Mussolini and the Fascists seized power. Though within a framework of legality, the Fascists were soon entrenched at all levels of government, and Mussolini assumed dictatorial control. His settlement with the church and his ability apparently to satisfy large sectors of the populace added to his strength and influence. The first fascist state would soon be ready for active and ultimately disruptive foreign adventures in the 1930s.

For both France and Great Britain the sweet taste of victory became bitter early after the war. The long struggle had disrupted many of those nations' economic enterprises and opened new avenues for political expression. The problems were more acute in France because that nation became the guardian of the Versailles Treaty. France's desire for security clouded much of her home life. The disillusionment, by 1923, sent French armies into the German Ruhr to force reparations payment. The German resistance, though passive, further aggravated the situation. For France, as for the rest of Europe, these were not easy times; but France's governments, like those of Great Britain, however frequently changed, still maintained control.

For Poland and the so-called successor states of the once Austro-Hungarian monarchy (Czechoslovakia, Hungary, Romania, Yugoslavia, Austria), the newly established independence was—except for Czechoslovakia and at times Austria—an impossible situation. Sudden independence, won as the war ended, fostered serious economic dislocation and bitter nationalist quarrels over territory and boundary lines. The problem of the nationalities, never resolved by the Dual Monarchy, proved no less troublesome for the successor states.

The Weimar Republic of Germany was saddled from the outset with an economic and psychological burden that it would not fully overcome. Impressively the government struggled to satisfy the German people and the victorious allies. The Ruhr invasion proved those efforts fruitless. Yet after 1923 there were strong signs, capped by the Locarno accords in 1925, that Germany, after all, would make it back into the "establishment" of European order.

All the political experimentation witnessed in what was America's "roaring" twenties would too quickly face the test of supreme financial disorder. As you will see in the next chapter, the Great Depression which began in 1929 would soon force European peoples to choose between their pursuit of liberal principles and the very security upon which their existence, if not well-being, depended.

Identifications

Identify each one of the following as used in the text. Refer to the text as necessary.

	Text page
"normalcy"	521
Cheka	520
Kronstadt Mutiny	520
Nikolai Bukharin	521
Twenty-one Conditions	521
Cartel des Gauches	525
Ramsay MacDonald	526
Sinn Fein	526
Josef Pilsudski	527
Thomas Masaryk	527
Engelbert Dollfuss	528
Corfu Agreement of 1927	528
General John Metaxas	528
Kapp Putsch	529
Twenty-five Points	531
Mein Kampf	531
Gustav Stresemann	531
Charles E. Dawes/Owen D. Young	531
Locarno Agreements of 1925	531-532

Map Exercise A

Locate each of the following bodies of water:

Adriatic Sea	Baltic Sea	Ionian Sea	North Sea
Aegean Sea	Black Sea	Ligurian Sea	the Skagerrak
Sea of Azov	Caspian Sea	Mediterranean Sea	Tyrrhenian Sea

Fill in or mark those countries that were created by circumstances occurring at the end of World War I.

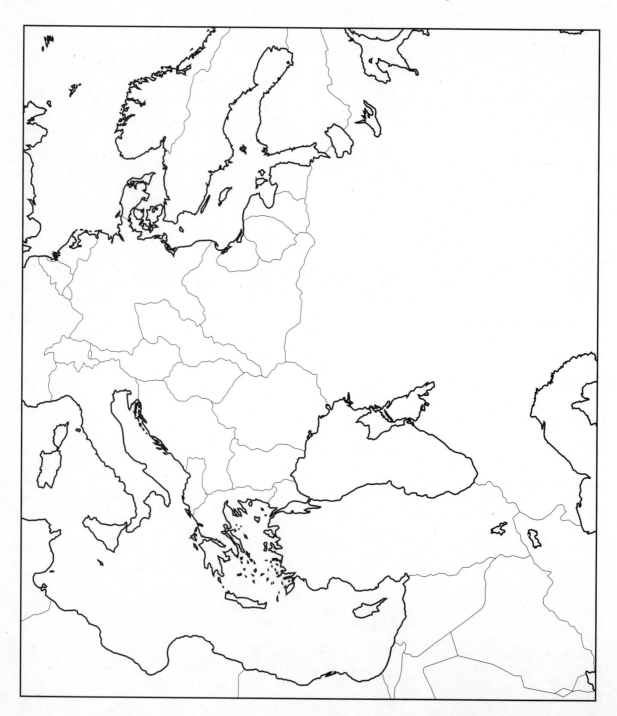

Map Exercise B

Mark the following cities and geographic points on this map of Russia.

Kiev
Moscow
Novgorod
St. Petersburg
Vladivostok
Yakutsk

Ural Mountains
Sakhalin Island
Siberia
Lake Baikal
Bering Sea
Aral Sea

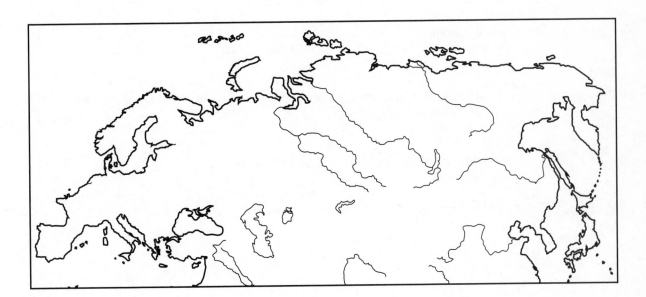

Short-Answer Exercises

Multiple-Choice

_____1. Attempts to revise the Treaty of Versailles normally stemmed from such problems as:
(a) nationalistic concerns
(b) inadequate enforcement of the Treaty
(c) demands for greater self-determination in eastern Europe
(d) all of these

_____2. One of the most significant social changes brought on by the war was the elevated position of particularly:
(a) the elderly
(b) disabled veterans
(c) labor unions
(d) all of these

_____3. As part of Lenin's New Economic Policy the government authorized private economic enterprise in which of the following?
(a) an open grain market
(b) private control of banking
(c) state control of every aspect of the Russian economy
(d) all of these

_____4. Stalin's strength seems to have been derived from the fact that he was:
(a) a master of administrative methods
(b) an excellent writer
(c) a gifted speaker
(d) witty and flashy

_____5. Which of the following is the most correct statement about Mussolini:
(a) he was always a nationalist
(b) he was always a socialist
(c) he originally was a socialist and became a nationalist during World War I
(d) he always put the nation before himself

_____6. Secret military connections were initiated between Germany and the Soviet Union as a result of the:
(a) Treaty of Rapallo
(b) Kellogg-Briand Pact
(c) Locarno Agreements
(d) Rentenmark

_____7. In 1918 the British electorate included:
(a) men aged twenty-one and women aged twenty-five
(b) only men
(c) men aged twenty-one and women aged thirty
(d) men and women aged twenty-one.

_____8. In the 1920s the Irish Civil War lingered on over the issue of:
(a) the six counties of Ulster
(b) the oath of allegiance to the monarchy
(c) Protestants within the Irish Free State
(d) neutrality in world affairs

_____9. The Weimar Republic's Constitution did each of the following, except:
(a) guaranteed civil liberties and provided for universal suffrage
(b) established the basis for proportional representation in the *Reichstag*
(c) severely curtailed Presidential authority
(d) gave greater power to the President in times of emergency

_____10. The original appeal of the Nazi party appears to have been to:
(a) the wealthy
(b) war veterans
(c) the communists
(d) Jews

True/False

_____1. In the spirit of political experimentation after the First World War, most countries attempted several democratic forms of government and then turned to authoritarianism.

_____2. Compared to the other ideologies of this era, Russian communists believed that Marxism-Leninism could be established throughout the world.

_____3. After the stringent economic policies of "War Communism," Lenin somewhat reversed his position with his sponsorship of the New Economic Policy.

_____4. Josef Stalin advocated the policy of "socialism in one country."

_____5. Between the end of World War I and January 1933, France was governed by more than twenty-five different cabinets.

_____6. Bela Kun, Miklos Horthy, Joseph Pilsudski and Kurt von Schuschnigg are all associated with the turbulent politics of Hungary during the post-war era.

_____7. The actual reparations "bill" presented to Germany by the Allies in 1921 amounted to 132 billion gold marks.

_____8. By 1922 Hitler and the Nazis were defining socialism along traditional German ideological lines.

_____9. The election of Paul von Hindenburg to the presidency in 1925 suggests an accommodation of conservative elements to the reality of the Weimar Republic.

_____10. The overall results of the many political experiments of the 1920s should be characterized as mixed at best.

Completion

1. The idea of the necessity of communist revolutions throughout the world would be associated with the name of _____ .

2. The general term of _____ is often used to describe the right-wing dictatorships that came into being before World War II.

3. _____ was the king of Italy from 1900 to 1946.

4. A sensational example of Mussolini's willingness to use force and violence appears in the murder of _____ .

5. Mussolini's settlement with the Roman Catholic Church in 1929 was known as the _____ .

6. The General Strike of 1926 in Great Britain began when _____ went out on strike.

7. During World War I the only national group to rise violently against a government was the _____ .

8. The only government carved out of the collapsed Austro-Hungarian Empire to avoid a form of authoritarian government after World War I was _____ .

9. During the Ruhr crisis of 1923 the American dollar was worth _____ German marks.

10. As a result of the agreements at _____ a new atmosphere of hope and optimism appeared throughout Europe.

For Further Consideration

1. The struggle for power between Leon Trotsky and Josef Stalin has long been a subject for study by students of Communist Russia. What were the chief issues that divided these two men? Can you envision other factors that may have entered into the struggle?

2. Describe the manner of the Fascist takeover in Italy in 1922. What were the historic forces operating that brought Mussolini to power? How would you assess Mussolini's abilities as a politician?

3. With attention to specific problems, compare and contrast the postwar situation in Great Britain and in France.

4. Compare and contrast the inter-war development of Poland, Hungary, Czechoslovakia (now the Czech Republic and Slovakia), and what is today the former Yugoslavia.

5. Using the points noted on pp. 631–632 of the textbook (from the Nazi Party's Twenty-five Points), comment on the political, social and economic implications of each.

Answers

Multiple-Choice

		Text page
1.	D	518
2.	C	518-519
3.	B	520
4.	A	521
5.	C	522
6.	A	525
7.	C	525
8.	D	526-27
9.	C	529
10.	C	531

True/False

1.	F	518
2.	T	519-520
3.	T	520
4.	T	521
5.	F	525
6.	F	528
7.	T	529
8.	F	531
9.	T	531
10.	T	532-533

Completion

1.	Leon Trotsky	521
2.	*fascist*	522
3.	Victor Emmanuel III	523
4.	Giacomo Matteotti	524
5.	Lateran Accord	524
6.	coalminers	526
7.	Irish	526
8.	Czechoslovakia	527
9.	800 million	529
10.	Locarno	532-533

28
Europe and the Great Depression of the 1930s

Commentary

The worldwide difficulties caused by the Depression, which began in 1929, cannot be fully appreciated. In reality it was the first time that modern era governments had to face the economic dislocations associated with near "total" war. The period of the 1920s and 1930s was the most serious disruption in European economic life since the advent of industrialization. Unemployment—as one-time soldiers flooded the postwar labor market faltering factory output—as industry was converted to peacetime production; severe fluctuation of the European financial structure—as the question of reparations remained unresolved and essentially unpaid: these were among the important consequences of World War I. Further compounded by national ambition and self-righteousness in the postwar era, these problems remained and by 1929 manifested themselves in the Great Depression. As time passed it was clear that the staggering cost of the war could not be borne by Germany through the ill-fated system of reparation payments. Yet France insisted on payment. Despite the problems, however, by the mid-1920s there was room for mild optimism. A reduction of reparation payment schedules and a growing atmosphere of trust, which was associated with the Locarno Conference in 1925, suggested that the "war" was finally over. The widespread development of new products like the radio and the automobile, coupled with new technological developments in synthetic production, further supported the optimistic mood.

But in the end the fragile economy of the West crashed. The largely unregulated speculation on America's stock exchanges created a ripple effect throughout the world's economy. Country after country would be forced to deal with the new circumstances created by the Great Depression.

Every nation of Europe, and the United States, was seriously affected. To this economic downturn every citizen, in one way or another, had to adjust his or her life. In all countries that were still democratic, assaults were being made on the parliamentary system of government. The totalitarian states—Germany, Russia, and Italy—were equally affected. Russia and Italy, however, had established systems of government that could go well beyond the normal restrictions imposed by the democracies, and Germany was in the process of doing so. In some cases organized and violent control over the citizenry allowed those countries to weather the economic crisis of the Depression. Their success was sometimes viewed as positive proof that totalitarianism was the future form of government for all of Europe.

Great Britain and France managed to survive by accepting political coalitions and economic ideas not dreamed of in the pre-war era. Italy's Mussolini never fully solved the problem of economic needs in his country and by 1935 resorted to international adventures to take pressure off Fascist failings at home.

Germany, the most severely struck by the Depression, fell into the grasp of Hitler and the Nazis, who never failed to brutally eliminate opponents, real or imagined. No one person, no group, not even an entire race of people could be secure against the open and organized assault on humanity witnessed during the Nazi era.

Although the facts are less visible in the U.S.S.R., there is little doubt that the vast economic reorganization of Russia instituted by Stalin caused an untold hardship on Soviet citizens. The industrial machine created by the Five Year Plans, and admired by many in the West, was oiled by the blood of millions. It is clear today that even with the passing of the Soviet Union as an economic entity, Russia's economic problems remain serious and deeply rooted. The economic hardships suffered by the Russian populace under the Czars and under communism continue to defy simple and quick solutions. And this regardless of western aid and the concomitant encouragement of capitalist style approaches there.

As a catastrophe of the Western world, the Great Depression taught many hard lessons. But before these could be fully realized, Europe had been pushed into World War II.

Identifications

Identify each one of the following as used in the text. Refer to text as necessary.

Map Exercise A

On the accompanying map, shade the areas of the world controlled by dictatorships in 1939.

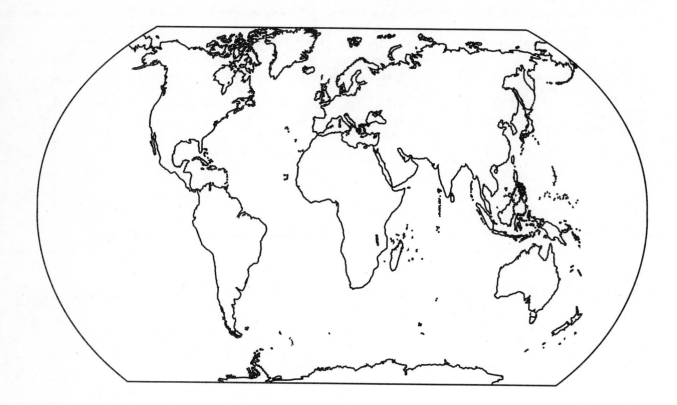

Map Exercise B

On this map of the European continent mark all of the countries of Europe with the approximate boundaries of 1939.

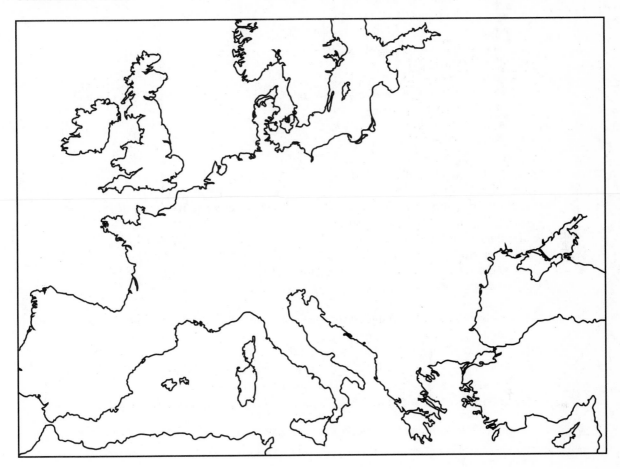

Short-Answer Exercises

Multiple-Choice

_____1. The world commodity market of the 1930s saw:
(a) food production surpass demand
(b) government-accumulated reserves at record levels
(c) the price of foodstuffs drop severely
(d) all of these

_____2. Who of the following agreed to form a coalition cabinet (the National Government) in an effort to fight the Depression?
(a) Stanley Baldwin
(b) Winston Churchill
(c) Neville Chamberlain
(d) Ramsay MacDonald

_____3. Right-wing groups in France such as the *Action Française* and the *Croix de Feu* were opposed to all of the following except:
(a) military rule
(b) socialism
(c) communism
(d) parliamentary rule

_____4. In which country did unemployment rise from 2,258,000 in March 1930 to over 6 million in March 1932?
(a) Germany
(b) Italy
(c) France
(d) Great Britain

_____5. By the 1930s the least likely support for the Nazi party within Germany came from:
(a) the young
(b) communists
(c) most intellectuals
(d) war veterans.

_____6. In what year were the Nuremberg Laws enacted?
(a) 1933
(b) 1935
(c) 1942
(d) 1944

_____7. Which of the following was not a part of Mussolini's economic program?
(a) importation of foreign grain supplies
(b) vast public works programs
(c) protective tariffs
(d) subsidies to industries

_____8. Between the years 1928 and 1940 Soviet industrial growth appears to have been near:
   (a) 100 percent
   (b) 400 percent
   (c) 200 percent
   (d) 50 percent

_____9. In 1930, claiming "Dizziness from success," this leader called a brief halt to the process of agricultural collectivization:
   (a) Lenin
   (b) Trotsky
   (c) Kirov
   (d) Stalin

_____10. Which of the following events occurred first?
   (a) Hindenburg defeats Hitler for the presidency of Germany
   (b) New York stock market collapses
   (c) assassination of Sergei Kirov
   (d) Reichstag fire

True/False

_____1. Disruption in the world marketplace and the financial crisis caused by the First World War led to the Great Depression.

_____2. In the years immediately after the war it was the United States that insisted upon repayment of war debts.

_____3. The idea of increasing government spending to offset the effects of the Depression is normally associated with British Prime Minister Ramsay MacDonald.

_____4. The National Government placated the populace by seeming to steer a middle course between the extremes of both the Labour and Conservative parties.

_____5. Léon Blum's leadership of the French Popular Front aimed at establishing a socialist and democratic government.

_____6. In the 1932 *Reichstag* elections saw the Nazi party gain a clear parliamentary majority.

_____7. Anti-Semitism became a key element of the Nazi program in Germany only after Hitler gained power in 1933.

_____8. Lenin's New Economic Policy firmly established the economic program of communism in the Soviet Union.

_____9. The State Planning Commission (Gosplan) had the overall responsibility for industrial planning in the Soviet Union.

_____10. The best estimate for the number of people executed and imprisoned as a result of Stalin's purges is in the hundreds of thousands.

Completion

1. The 1931 moratorium on all international debt was initiated by the American President
   _____ .

2. _____ wrote the *General Theory of Employment, Interest, and Money.*

3. In 1931 a British political coalition of Labor, Conservative, and Liberal ministers formed the so-called _____ .

4. The _____ is a name given to the small group of advisers to Weimar President Hindenburg.

5. After the incident of the _____ the German *Reichstag* allowed Hitler to rule by decree.

6. As a result of the death of _____ Hitler was able to combine the offices of chancellor and president into one.

7. By 1936 _____ was in charge of all police functions in Germany.

8. _____ was the 1935 series of laws passed against German Jews and their institutions.

9. _____ was the country invaded by Italy in 1935.

10. _____ is the word used to describe the agricultural reorganization of Russia under Stalin.

For Further Consideration

1. Describe the politics surrounding and the reform policies of Leon Blum and the Popular Front in France.

2. In an examination of German political maneuvering between 1930 and Hitler's appointment as Chancellor in 1933, what factors, beyond the clearly economic, seem to have undermined the Weimar Republic?

3. Using both Italian and German examples, describe the economic system of fascism, or corporatism. Generally, what was the fascist view of private property and of capital?

4. Describe the causes, aims, and effects of the Stalinist purges.

5. In your opinion why were the ruthless policies of the dictatorships of the 1930s possible? Why were they so often successful?

Answers

Multiple-Choice

		Text page
1.	D	536-537
2.	B	539
3.	A	539
4.	A	541
5.	C	542
6.	B	543
7.	A	543
8.	B	545
9.	D	545
10.	D	546

True/False

1.	T	536
2.	T	536
3.	F	537
4.	T	539
5.	T	540
6.	F	541
7.	F	543
8.	F	544-545
9.	T	544-545
10.	F	545

Completion

1.	Herbert Hoover	536
2.	John Maynard Keynes	537
3.	National Government	539
4.	Hindenburg Circle	541-542
5.	Reichstag Fire	542
6.	President Hindenburg	543
7.	Heinrich Himmer	543
8.	Nuremberg Laws	543
9.	Ethiopia	544
10.	Collectivization	544

29
World War II

Commentary

The answers to complex historical questions and/or situations are never easy to assess. This most certainly is true of the wars of the twentieth century. They are close to us in time, and continue to affect the world in which we live. The roots of World War I were embedded in the nineteenth century and earlier; those of World War II lie there as well and in the events surrounding the 1914–1918 war. Unquestionably the Great Depression was a factor that further fostered circumstances and decisions not contemplated in an earlier era. However, the normal historical evaluation of the origins of World War II are made even more difficult by at least two other factors. Both reflect the inescapable problem of human life in general and the contemporary nature of the event which ended just over fifty years ago. First, the Nazi racial program of mass extermination of many different peoples and the outright genocide against European Jews is one nearly incomprehensible factor, almost defying explanation. Second, in our own time we continue to experience problems relating to the war, to the succeeding Cold War, and now post-Cold War conditions.

It is clear that conditions in Europe between the wars coupled with aggressive totalitarian nationalism were major causes of the war. Real and perceived injustices, the collapse of the concept of collective security, and uncertain and often indecisive national policies represent additional factors. However broad these characteristics of the inter-war years may appear to us, the road to World War II has a deliberate direction. Without question the Weimar Republic was the most strained by the world war that ended in 1918. Awakened nationalism and heightened socioeconomic problems were parlayed by the Nazi Party into complete control of Germany. Becoming Chancellor in 1933, Adolf Hitler was in a position to bring his ideas and former pronouncements into being. By the early 1930s the post-war hope for a peace sponsored by the newly formed League of Nations collapsed as Japan invaded Manchuria (1931), and Italy attacked Ethiopia (1935). A crucial test for France came in March 1936 when German troops re-occupied the Rhineland in deliberate violation of the Versailles Treaty and the Locarno Pacts of 1925. The failure to act against this blatant disregard for solemn agreements only increased the appetite of the augmentative dictators. Hitler and Mussolini supported the rebels in Spain which allowed a fascist government under General Francisco Franco to emerge there in 1939. The Nazis brought increasing pressures against Austria and Czechoslovakia. A near-war in the spring of 1938 over the Sudetenland of Czechoslovakia set the stage for the effective destruction of the most successful of the central European states created at the end of World War I. The Munich Conference averted immediate war, but emboldened Hitler and left England and France apparently cowered, and sent Italy further into Hitler's embrace. In a surprise move the communist state of the Soviet Union and the fascist state of Germany became strange bedfellows indeed, by signing the Nazi-Soviet Pact of 1939, sealing Poland's fate.

World War II was on. For the first time in human history war was truly global. Destruction raged across three continents (Europe, Asia, and Africa) and over and under vast oceans. From the invasion of

Poland in September 1939 to the collapse of France in the summer of 1941, the Germans experienced complete success in their military conquests. But Churchill's Britain would not yield. The German air attack there proved futile, while Hitler's support of Mussolini's faltering legions in Africa and the Balkans delayed the massive assault into Russia. By the end of 1941 two significant factors were beginning to operate. The German offensive in Russia had been stopped before Moscow, changing the character of the war in the east, and Imperial Japan launched a surprise air attack against American ships and naval facilities at Hawaii, quickly bringing the United States into World War II. By 1943, though far from over, and with Italy out of the picture, the war's direction was being governed by the Allies. Russian pressures in the east and the Normandy invasion in mid-1944 put the Germans almost totally on the defensive. By May 1945, with the war over in Europe, two nuclear attacks on their cities brought Japan's formal surrender in September of that year. The Second "Great" War of this century was over, and with it European domination of the planet came to an end.

Exemplified by a wartime series of head-of-state "summit-type" meetings, the mutual distrust of the Western democracies and communist Russia was only temporarily suspended, and never totally. In the power vacuum thus created the U.S. (United States) and the S.U. (Union of Soviet Socialist Republics) moved from a reluctant partnership of the wartime era to being global adversaries shortly after the war concluded.

It is this post-World War II juxtaposition of global power that emerged as the dominant factor of the last half-century and molded the contemporary posture of the Western state system. Remarkably, as the early 1990s have already shown, the world created out of the ruins of World War II is changing dramatically in a direction no one could at this moment predict.

Today it is even clearer, as more once-secret information becomes available, that the tension of Cold War politics started before the bombs stopped falling. It is this Cold War that has effectively dominated the scene since the end of World War II. Much controversy surrounds the origins of the Cold War.

Unclear intentions, expansionist motives, growing mistrust, and Stalinist support of communist parties in eastern Europe all contributed to the post World War II atmosphere. The end of the war left too many unresolved international and colonial problems for the infant United Nations to deal with. Too much physical and psychological damage, too much an upset to established order, too much tension had developed for any easy solution. With much less notice at the time, the world had passed into the nuclear age. The nations of the world and those peoples seeking nationhood in the wake of the Second World War faced too many uncertainties after 1945—uncertainties that are now a part of the contemporary Western heritage.

Identifications

Identify each one of the following as used in the text. Refer to the text as necessary.

Map Exercise A

1. Outline the area known as the Sudetenland of Czechoslovakia.
2. Draw a line showing the areas of concentration of Czech and Slovak peoples.
3. Locate the city of Prague on the map.
4. Locate Poland; show the so-called "Polish Corridor" dividing Germany in 1939.
5. Locate the Baltic states of Latvia, Estonia, Lithuania, and Finland.
6. Locate each of the following cities: Berlin, Warsaw, Danzig, and Helsinki.

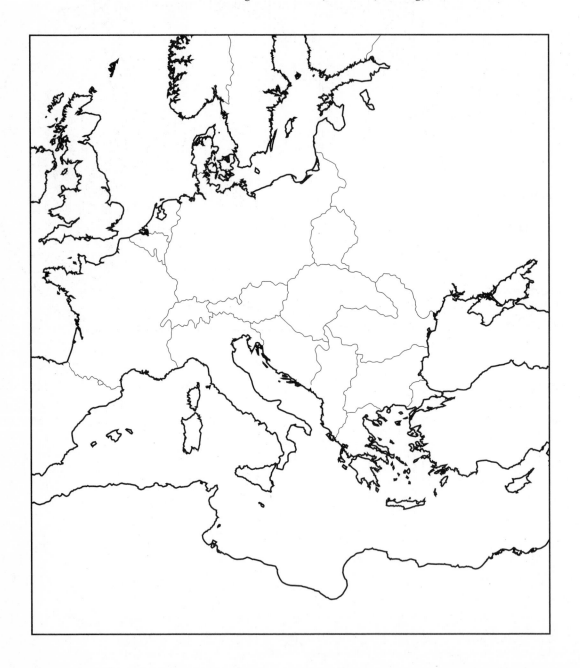

Map Exercise B

On this world map mark the major battle lines/fronts and battles of World War II on land and at sea.

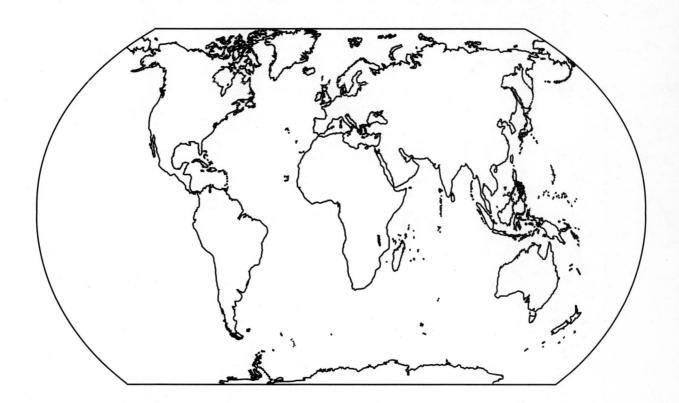

Short-Answer Exercises

Multiple-Choice

_____1. Which of the following represents the best explanation for the 1935 Italian invasion of
Ethiopia?
(a) to divert attention from economic conditions in Italy
(b) the need to avenge the Italian defeat there in 1896
(c) the desire to restore the glory of ancient Rome
(d) all of these

_____2. The establishment of the Spanish Republic in 1931 brought to power a government that
supported:
(a) the Catholic Church
(b) separatists and radicals
(c) large landowners
(d) none of these

_____3. After the Munich agreement, who declared that he had made a "peace with honor"?
(a) Benito Mussolini
(b) Neville Chamberlain
(c) Konrad Henlein
(d) Adolf Hitler, when he renounced further territorial demands in Europe

_____4. _____ contributed to Winston Churchill's success as a British leader.
(a) His ability as a writer and speaker
(b) his confidence in Britain
(c) his attitude toward British nationalism
(d) all of these

_____5. German racial policies were least applied in:
(a) Norway
(b) Russia
(c) Poland
(d) the Slavic countries in general

_____6. _____ would be considered along with Nazi Germany as unmatched in
the committing of atrocities.
(a) Italy
(b) The Soviet Union
(c) Hungary
(d) Romania

_____7. The 1945 "Battle of the Bulge" had the effect of showing that:
(a) Germany would soon lose the war
(b) years of tough fighting might possibly lie ahead
(c) Japan was finished
(d) American soldiers were no match for the Germans

_____8. Which of the following statements best describes the reasons behind the decision to use the atomic bomb?
(a) it was unnecessary to win the war, but it would teach the yellow races a lesson
(b) the use of the bomb by the United States would make the Russians more cooperative after the war
(c) it was a way to end the war and save American lives
(d) the decision was not thought out at all

_____9. During World War II German women were:
(a) portrayed as docile helpmates
(b) forbidden to have sexual relations with non-Germans
(c) not allowed to work in munitions factories
(d) only permitted agriculturally related jobs

_____10. As Woodrow Wilson was in an earlier era, President Franklin Roosevelt was:
(a) suspicious of British motives
(b) to place great faith in an international organization
(c) willing to make considerable compromises
(d) all of these

True/False

_____1. Falangists were members of the pro-fascist parties opposing the Spanish Popular Front government in the Civil War there.

_____2. After signing the Munich agreements in September 1938, Hitler believed that it was "peace with honor."

_____3. One of the reasons behind the Nazi-Soviet Pact, secretly aimed at the division of Poland, was Stalin's distrust of the English and French after not being consulted over the partition of Czechoslovakia the previous year.

_____4. The French government which accepted defeat at the hands of the Germans ironically was led by a former World War I military hero.

_____5. Fighting in North Africa against both the British and later the Americans earned German General Erwin Rommel the accolade of "The Desert Fox."

_____6. In late 1941 General Tojo led the Japanese militarists toward war with the United States.

_____7. The goal of American forces "island hopping" campaign was to recapture every island that Japan held in the Pacific.

_____8. That Japan could keep Hirohito as emperor was the only condition under which Japan surrendered to the United States in August of 1945.

_____9. In general, Vichy France tended toward liberal excesses.

_____10. The British Broadcasting Company (BBC) used propaganda to further the war effort, urging resistance to the Nazis in programs transmitted abroad in all European languages.

Completion

1. Nazi expansionist policies required the conquest of _____ and the _____.

2. Haunted by the _____ of the last war, neither Great Britain nor France was willing to respond to Hitler's earlier provocations.

3. In 1936 General _____ led the revolt against the Spanish Popular Front.

4. In the late 1930s many of Adolf Hitler's gains came as a result of the British Prime Minister Neville Chamberlain's policy of _____ .

5. Within Nazi Germany's racial theory the Slavic peoples were considered subhuman creatures known in German as _____ .

6. The German word _____ means "purified of Jews."

7. The first reversal of Axis progress in World War II came with the American naval victories in the battles of _____ and _____ .

8. The turning point of the Russian campaign came with the battle of _____ during the winter of 1942–1943.

9. The first meeting of the wartime allies (Churchill, Roosevelt, and Stalin) took place in _____ .

10. _____ was the only representative of the three major victorious powers who could attend both the Yalta and Potsdam Conferences.

For Further Consideration

1. Discuss the Munich Agreement of 1938. Outline the position of the states directly involved. Does this settlement contain any lessons for the contemporary world?

2. Discuss the questions surrounding high-altitude bombing during World War II. What were the primary and secondary targets? Was this method effective? Do the lessons learned in precision bombing during World War II have any effect on us today?

3. Suppose that the Nazis had not adopted the racial policies that they did. In your opinion, would the outcome of World War II have been any different? If the outcome had been the same, how might historians have come to judge the rise and fall of Adolf Hitler?

4. Considering the respective backgrounds of World War I and World War II, compare and contrast the founding of the League of Nations with the founding of the United Nations.

5. Discuss Stalin's policies and leadership throughout this period. In your opinion was Russia's position respective to the rise of Nazism equally responsible for the war? Answer with specific details as needed.

Answers

Multiple-Choice

		Text page
1.	D	551
2.	D	552
3.	B	554
4.	D	556
5.	A	559
6.	B	560
7.	A	563
8.	C	564
9.	D	565
10.	D	569

True/False

1.	T	551
2.	F	552
3.	T	554
4.	T	556
5.	T	559
6.	T	560
7.	F	563
8.	T	564
9.	F	565
10.	T	569

Completion

1.	Poland/Ukraine	551
2.	memories	552
3.	Francisco Franco	552
4.	appeasement	552, 554
5.	untermenschen	559
6.	Judenrein	559
7.	Coral Sea; Midway Island	561
8.	Stalingrad	561
9.	Tehran, Iran	569
10.	Josef Stalin	569-570

30
Faces of the Twentieth Century:
European Social Experiences

Commentary

The Second World War was an event that politically divided the twentieth century, closing the era of European world domination and opening the era of Cold War conflict between the United States and the Soviet Union, which ended with the collapse of Communism. The war, however, did not constitute a major divide in European social history. Rather it was an event of enormous destruction during a century that witnessed the unleashing of destructive military and political forces that shaped and reshaped much of the social experience of Europe.

Historians have tended to regard social history as primarily a study of private life lived largely outside the concerns of politics and the state. Indeed, social historians many years ago, though less so today, often defined their work as standing more or less in opposition to political, diplomatic, and military history. When, however, one turns to the social history of Europe in the twentieth century that distinction is difficult, if not impossible to maintain. To separate the lives of the mass of twentieth-century Europeans from the political and military events of the era would falsify any account of their personal lives as they lived them. Consequently, the intermeshing of social and political history will feature more prominently than it has in our previous considerations of social experience.

During the first half of the twentieth century, the groups whose personal and social lives were most dramatically reshaped—as a result of radical transformations imposed by authoritarian governments—were women Soviet peasants, and central and Eastern European Jews. Each of their stories might stand as an independent section of the history of the dictatorships or of the events of World War II, but that approach would separate them from their place in the larger fabric of European social experience determined by the forces of state violence.

In the first two decades of the twentieth century, the lives of European women expanded considerably. In many parts of Europe, universities and the professions had opened to women of the upper class. Elsewhere in the social structure, the growth of office work and public school systems created new economic opportunities for women. World War I marked a major moment of significant—if not always permanent—transformation, as thousands of women entered the workforce to replace the men who were fighting the war. Many women could now imagine social roles for themselves in addition to those of wives and mothers. The war also saw greater sexual freedom and experimentation. After the war, women also entered more fully into the political life of Europe. In the face of these advances, despite enormous differences in their ideologies, the policies of the authoritarian governments of the Soviet Union, Italy, and Germany placed new constraints on women's lives even while giving them some paternalistic protections. In each nation, various political rhetorics described new roles for women, but each of those rhetorics collided with the realities of the economy, politics, and everyday life.

With regard to Soviet peasant life, the collectivization of farming, the rapid industrialization, and the purges that occurred in the Soviet Union during the 1930s touched every part of Soviet society. However, these forces particularly shaped the lives of Soviet peasants who were confronted with poor living conditions in the country and in the cities, and enormous peasant flight from the land to the cities, and ongoing shortage of the most basic consumer goods, such as food, clothing, and shoes. But for much of the century, the Soviet people sustained themselves in the face of these difficulties mainly through the convictions that they were enduring their present troubles to build a greater socialist future in which the world would be set right and all the goods people needed would be available. During World War II, this emphasis changed to protecting the fatherland. After the war, the emphasis again fell on a better future, but that future never came.

A large Jewish community had dwelled within Polish lands for centuries, often in a climate of religious and cultural anti-Semitism. During the interwar years, the Polish government pursued policies that were directly anti-Semitic and because Jews filled a disproportionate number of jobs in commerce, any legislation affecting such occupations such as shopkeeping, peddling, and crafts disproportionally touched their lives. However, it was not until the joint German-Soviet invasion of Poland that millions of Jews were brought under German or Soviet authority, and the plan of Hitler and his "final solution" was put into effect. The Nazi Germany government first thought that it might herd virtually all Jews into one region, and many Jews were moved into ghettos. By 1941, the Polish Jews had lost all their civic standing and property.

The outbreak of the war between Germany and the Soviet Union in June 1941 further transformed the situation of Jews in Poland. The advancing German forces killed tens of thousands of Jews in the Soviet Union during 1941, and the Nazi government decided to exterminate the Jews of Europe, and transported Jews from the ghettos by rail to a series of death camps located in Poland. The Nazi authorities regarded this process as a major part of their "final solution" to the Jewish question.

The twentieth century was the most destructive in human history. The wars of the first half of the century destroyed the lives of millions of Europeans and disrupted the fabric of European society across the continent. The authoritarian governments of the Bolsheviks, Fascists, and National Socialists sought to remake whole societies according to utopian visions that resulted in political repressions, death, and social relocation of numerous minority groups. All of these ideologically driven governments sharply circumscribed the lives of women. Never before in European history and such a vast scheme as the collectivization of Soviet agriculture been undertaken in so short a time or with such disregard for law and human rights. The radical ideology of National Socialism led to the attempt to destroy the Jews of Europe and eradicated virtually all the Jewish community in Poland as well as those in other regions under Nazi control. The Holocaust stands as much as part of the social experience of this century as a part of its political history.

By the close of the century Europe, like much of the rest of the world, had entered a new age of technological revolution through the computer and improved health through advances in medical care. Economic growth slowed in the last decade of the century, but most of Europe outside former communist-dominated regions continued to enjoy a high standard of living under liberal democratic governments. In the regions of the former Soviet Union and its empire, the challenge became how to realize economic growth in some form of market economy without the former centralized state planning.

Identifications

Identify each one of the following as used in the text. Refer to text as necessary.

	text page
Alexandra Kollantai	574
"Soviet Man," "Soviet Woman"	573
Bundists	580
Clement Attlee	582
British Labour Party and the German Social Democratic Party	581-582
Simone de Beauvoir	583
The Third International	584
Soren Kierkegaard	584
Martin Heidegger	585
"americanization"	586
The Greens	587
Karl Barth	588
Honest to God	588
Pope Paul VI	588-589
Karol Wojtyla	589
"haves," "have nots"	590

Short-Answer Exercises

Multiple-Choice

_____1. During the first half of the twentieth century the groups whose personal and social lives were most dramatically reshaped as a result of the radical transformations imposed by authoritarian governments were all but:
(a) women
(b) children
(c) Soviet peasants
(d) Eastern European Jews

_____2. Soon after achieving power in late 1917, the_____ began issuing laws pertaining to women.
(a) Falangists
(b) Communists
(c) Socialists
(d) Bolsheviks

_____3. During Mussolini's fascist regime _____ of the Italian workforce was women.
(a) 10%
(b) 20%
(c) 25%
(d) 50%

_____4. About what percent of Polish Jews survived the Nazi Holocaust?
(a) 10
(b) 20
(c) 5
(d) 40

_____5. Which of the following was not the site of a Nazi concentration camp in Poland?
(a) Treblinka
(b) Dachau
(c) Sobibor
(d) Birkenau

_____6. All of the following led to a marked change in how numerous Europeans thought about social welfare except:
(a) decolonization
(b) the rise of authoritarian states
(c) World War II
(d) The Great Depression

_____7. The first European state to create a welfare state was:
(a) Germany
(b) Finland
(c) Italy
(d) Great Britain

_____8. Simone de Beauvoir is the author of:
    (a) Spare Rib
    (b) Courage Emma
    (c) Women for Women
    (d) The Second Sex

_____9. During the 1930s throughout Europe, students in the universities were often affiliated with what political party?
    (a) Communist
    (b) Democratic
    (c) Republican
    (d) none of these

_____10. Which of the following philosophers was deeply compromised by his association with the Nazis?
    (a) Jaspers
    (b) Heidegger
    (c) Sartre
    (d) Camus

True/False

_____1. Alexandra Kollontai took a very conservative, traditional view regarding the roles of women and men.

_____2. Mussolini wanted Italian women to have more children and remain at home to rear them.

_____3. During the 1920s, throughout much of the Soviet Union, the New Economic Policy led to a general failure regarding small commerce.

_____4. One of the fallouts of Soviet collectivization was an enormous peasant flight from the land to the cities.

_____5. Jews were among the wealthiest residents of Poland at the end of World War I.

_____6. World War II created a refugee problem and many people were displaced in central and Eastern Europe as well as the Soviet Union.

_____7. Before the construction of the Berlin Wall, an estimated 3 million East Germans migrated to West Germany via Berlin.

_____8. The most influential feminist thinker of the postwar period was the French intellectual, Simone de Beauvoir.

_____9. Heidegger was one of the major French existential writers.

_____10. American rock music is an example of the Americanization of European culture.

Completion

1. Like Italy's fascists, the Nazis wanted to increase their country's population, but they also wanted to guard Germany's _____ .

2. Despite the Fascists' claim that families should be supported by their male members, _____ percent of the Italian workforce was female.

3. During the interwar years, the Polish government pursued policies that were directly _____ .

4. The Nazi authorities considered the process of extermination of Jews to be a major part of their _____ .

5. Before World War II, except in _____, the two basic models for social legislation were the German and the British.

6. In Eastern Europe, under communism well over _____ percent of women were in the work force.

7. During the late 1920s and 1930s, _____ became a substitute religion for some Europeans.

8. Four events contributed to the eventual disillusionment of most European intellectuals with Soviet communism: the purges of the late 1930s; _____; the 1939 alliance between Russian and Germany; and the 1956 Soviet invasion of Hungary.

9. _____ was the country invaded by Italy in 1935.

10. The _____ movement originated among the radical student groups of the later 1960s and was concerned with the environment.

For Further Consideration

1. Describe the laws that the Bolsheviks issued that pertained to women. How did these laws affect women? In the late 1920s, what events precipitated the disruption of Soviet family life?

2. Discuss Mussolini's attitude toward women and how this attitude reflected his policy in Italy. How did Mussolini's policies reflect fascist thought overall?

3. In your opinion, how did the collectivization of farming, the rapid industrialization, and the purges that occurred in the Soviet Union during the 1930s profoundly shape Soviet individuals' social experiences?

4. In your opinion, could oppression and extermination of a certain ethnic group happen in the United States today? If so, what do you think would be the reaction of the general population? Has there been a time in American history when this type of oppression has occurred?

5. Discuss the intellectual movement known as existentialism. Who were some of the major writers who embraced this movement? How did their thoughts and writing reflect the happenings of the mid-twentieth century?

Answers

Multiple-Choice

		Text page
1.	B	573
2.	D	574
3.	C	575
4.	A	577
5.	B	580-581
6.	A	581-582
7.	D	582
8.	D	583
9.	A	584
10.	B	585

True/False

1.	F	574
2.	T	575
3.	F	576
4.	T	576
5.	F	577
6.	T	581
7.	T	581
8.	T	583
9.	F	585
10.	T	586

Completion

1.	racial purity	575
2.	25	575
3.	anti-Semitic	577
4.	"final solution"	580
5.	Scandinavia	581
6.	50	583
7.	Communism	584
8.	the Spanish Civil War	584
9.	Ethiopia	584
10.	German Green	587

31
The Cold War and the Emergence of the New Europe

Commentary

Today it is even clearer, as more once-secret information has become available, that the tension of Cold War politics actually started before the bombs stopped falling in World War II. It was this "Cold War" that effectively dominated most global events at least into the 1970s. The current trend is to accept that this Cold War, which had so long fashioned international competition between the United States and the Soviet Union, has ended. However, be mindful that much controversy surrounds the origins and direction of this postwar condition. Unclear intentions, expansionist motives, growing mistrust, and Stalinist support of communist parties in eastern Europe, as well as corresponding support by the United States for democratic (anti-communist) governments in western Europe, all contributed to the strained atmosphere of those first decades after World War II. United States-sponsored initiatives for the end of European controls over vast areas of Asia and Africa further complicated the scene after World War II. With victory U.S. trade and commerce, supported by sustained economic growth during and after the war, was soon global in character and influence. The Europeanization of the world that had started in the last century rapidly became, at least into the 1980s, a period of "Americanization."

The end of the war left too many unresolved international and colonial problems for the infant United Nations to deal with. That international organization, the successor of the League of Nations, despite all good intentions, was not able to positively influence the international and regional rivalries wrought by the war. The end of World War II left too much physical and psychological damage, too much of an upset to established order, and too much international tension for easy or cooperative solutions.

In the summer of 1945 the world, as a result of the United States' development and utilization of atomic bombs to end the war in Asia, passed into the nuclear age.

Contemporaneously, the nations of the world and those peoples seeking nationhood in the wake of World War II faced many uncertainties and a compelling need to rebuild. They had to reconstruct physical damage and needed to reevaluate and reorganize their sense of national and regional destiny. This process has continued into the present era against a backdrop of the Cold War, decolonization in Africa and Asia, and international uncertainty. Within this broad context intermittent strategic arms talks between the U.S. and the S.U. often have been viewed as a key barometer of East-West relations.

In the last decade there has been a relaxation of tension between the superpowers; but this seeming calm from time to time has been punctuated by regional crises.

However, in the period immediately following the war's end, Soviet expansionism in Europe and the establishment of communist government in China were catalysts for the "containment" policy fostered by the United States. Fear of the spread of communism across the ruins of Europe and Asia nurtured American programs such as the Truman Doctrine and the Marshall Plan. Narrowly averting war in

Germany in 1948, the Cold War heated up on the Korean Peninsula when a Russian-supported communist North Korea invaded South Korea. The formation of NATO and the police action in Korea capped the first round of the Cold War, which came to and end in 1953 with Stalin's death and the Korean armistice.

Without question World War II precipitated, and in some instances hastened, the withdrawal of European states from their former colonial territories. The process was rarely a smooth one, and residual bitterness remains. When Great Britain pulled out of the Indian subcontinent, several rival states were necessarily formed along religious lines. The transition to independence in Africa has rarely been without bloodshed. Here today there is continued evidence of bitter tribal struggles have threatened to take man's inhumanity to new heights. Decolonization for their former colonies in Indochina was painfully resisted by the French, and ultimately drew the United States into the region in a Cold War struggle against communism in Vietnam. Only now are U.S.-Vietnamese relations showing signs of what might be approaching normalcy.

The bold initiatives of the Reagan-Bush presidencies, such as the Strategic Defense Initiative and the American-supported United Nations defense of Kuwait, effectively ended the Cold War era and with growing uncertainties ushered in an era of collective security in which the United Nations is poised to play an important role.

Although less is known of the Soviet side of things, the end of the Korean conflict coupled with Stalin's death in 1953 created a brief period of uncertainty there that ended with the emergence of Nikita Khrushchev as the new Soviet leader. His government tried to take the Soviet Union to new domestic and international heights, but very well may have started the process that eventuated the end of the Marxist-Leninist (and Stalinist) dictatorship there. In retrospect, the Cuban Missile Crisis was the most dangerous moment in the Cold War. While the threat of a nuclear holocaust loomed at the time (1962), it is only recently that the world has learned (from previously secret Soviet documents) just how close it was.

Since the 1990s it has seemed apparent that a new world, fashioned out of the Cold War arena, has been emerging. Vast changes in eastern Europe, unheard of a decade ago, have occurred with the encouragement of the now defunct Soviet Union. Stirred by the reform program of leader Gorbachev, and then under President Boris Yeltsin, the former Soviet Union, which was reconstituted as the Commonwealth of Independent States (C.I.S.), has been engaged in a major restructuring program of its entire political and economic system. Constructive political and economic change and the hoped-for material progress appear as key goals in this effort.

On the one hand the collapse of Soviet control over Eastern Europe ushered in a period of unprecedented change there. For the western states the first cautious steps toward European integration have been taken. The European Economic Community has taken on a new life in what is no longer post-war Europe.

One of the most complex and long-standing trouble spots has been the Middle East. Here the violent mixture of Cold War politics, decolonization, and bitter religious hatred, coupled with the natural resource (oil) of the region, has created a caldron of local and regional rivalries. The abortive invasion (August 1990) of Kuwait by neighboring Iraq represents one of the most current examples. Add to this the establishment of the state of Israel, and the subsequent wars that erupted in the region since 1948, and the Middle East, even as the Cold War wanes, must remain high on the list of potential world trouble spots.

Identifications

Identify each one of the following as used in the text. Refer to the text as necessary.

	Text page
Vyacheslav Molotov	595
"Iron Curtain" speech	595
"containment" policy	595
Cominform	595
Theodore Herzl	597
Mao Tse-Tung	598
Khrushchev's "secret speech"	599
Gamal Abdel Nasser	599
Wladyslaw Gomulka	600
"peaceful coexistence"	600
Prague Spring	601
Ho Chi Minh	602
Ngo Dinh Diem	603
Margaret Thatcher	602
Charles de Gaulle	602, 605
EEC	605
Common Market	605
Helsinki Accords	606
Strategic Defense Initiative	608
Lech Walesa	607, 609
General Wojciech Jaruzelski	607, 609
Perestroika	608
Glasnost	608
Commonwealth of Independent States	612
Boris Yeltsin	612

Map Exercise A

On the accompanying map of the Korean Peninsula locate each of the following:

1. 38th parallel
2. Seoul
3. Pyongyang
4. Chosan

5. Pusan
6. Inchon
7. Panmunjom
8. 1953 armistice line

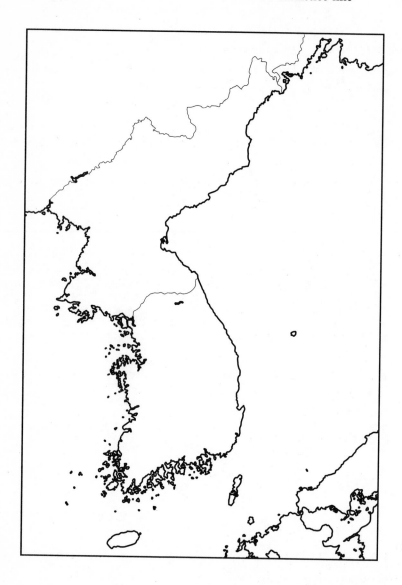

Map Exercise B

On the accompanying map of Southeast Asia locate each of the following:

1. Laos
2. Thailand
3. Cambodia (Khmer Republic)
4. North/South Vietnam
5. Bangkok
6. Phnom Penh
7. Saigon (Ho Chi Minh City)

8. Dien Bien Phu
9. Hanoi
10. Haiphong
11. Gulf of Tonkin
12. Hue
13. Pleiku
14. Mekong delta

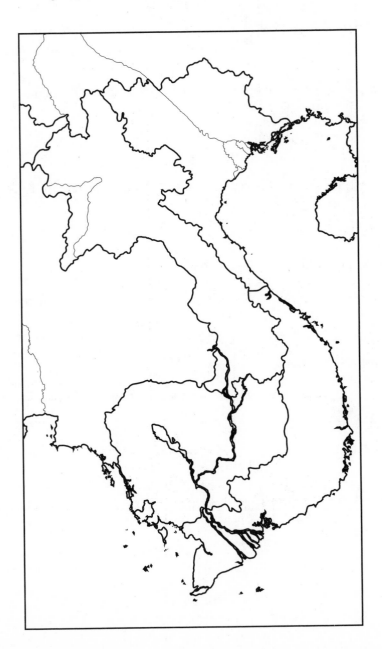

Short-Answer Exercises

Multiple-Choice

_____1. The Marshall Plan can be considered:
   (a) a complete failure
   (b) only moderately successful
   (c) a great success
   (d) neither a success nor a failure

_____2. Which is the correct post-World War II order for these presidents of the United States?
   (a) Ford, Carter, Nixon, Reagan, Bush
   (b) Eisenhower, Kennedy, Johnson, Ford, Nixon
   (c) Truman, Eisenhower, Kennedy, Ford, Reagan
   (d) Johnson, Kennedy, Nixon, Ford, Reagan

_____3. Which is the correct post-World War II order for these leaders of the Soviet Union?
   (a) Andropov, Khrushchev, Brezhnev, Gorbachev
   (b) Stalin, Khrushchev, Yeltsin, Gorbachev
   (c) Chernenko, Khrushchev, Brezhnev, Andropov
   (d) none of these

_____4. Russian Premier Khrushchev's abrupt ending of the 1960 Summit Conference at Paris was caused mainly by:
   (a) an unsatisfactory settlement of the Berlin issue
   (b) the Cuban Missle Crisis
   (c) the U-2 incident
   (d) his demand for President Eisenhower's resignation

_____5. The "most dangerous days" of the Cold War thus far are usually associated with the:
   (a) Korean War
   (b) construction of the Berlin Wall
   (c) Cuban Missile Crisis
   (d) American intervention in Vietnam

_____6. _____ is considered to have been the most powerful Russian leader since Stalin's era.
   (a) Alexei Kosygin
   (b) Nikita Khrushchev
   (c) Leonid Brezhnev
   (d) Lavrenti Beria

_____7. The strike in _____ was the catalyst for change in Poland, and led to a change in political leadership.
   (a) Leningrad
   (b) Warsaw
   (c) St. Petersburg
   (d) Gdansk

_____8. During his presidency, Reagan intensified Cold War rhetoric and proposed a new Strategic Arms Defense Initiative, known as:
(a) Star Wars
(b) the Evil Empire
(c) the Marshall Plan
(d) glasnost

_____9. After the resignation of the communist government in Czechoslovakia, who was elected president?
(a) Lech Walesa
(b) Helmut Kohl
(c) Janos Kada
(d) Vaclav Havel

_____10. After NATO air strikes in the former Yugoslavia, a peace agreement was signed in 1995 in what city?
(a) Washington, D.C.
(b) Gdansk, Poland
(c) Helsinki, Finland
(d) Dayton, Ohio

True/False

_____1. In 1946 Winston Churchill delivered his famed "Iron Curtain" speech to a joint session of the Congress of the United States.

_____2. In enunciating the Truman Doctrine in 1947 the President implied that the United States would support free peoples against aggression everywhere in the world.

_____3. The concept of the "Iron Curtain" is associated with the Roosevelt administration.

_____4. The Suez incident proved that even without U.S. support, the nations of western Europe were still perfectly capable of using military force to impose their will on the rest of the world.

_____5. Nationalist movements, colonial revolts, and Cold War politics are all factors in the so-called decolonization movement.

_____6. In November 1963, the same month that American President Kennedy was assassinated, South Vietnamese President Diem was murdered in an army coup that the United States may have encouraged.

_____7. American involvement in Southeast Asia throughout the 1960s allowed western European states to question American power and influence, and eroded the position of United States leadership of the free world.

_____8. The democratic socialist parties prospered after the onset of the Cold War.

_____9. The members of the Common Market sought to achieve the elimination of tariffs, a free flow of labor and capital, and similar wage and social benefits in all the participating countries.

_____10. Under President Jimmy Carter, the United States began a policy of detente with the Soviet Union.

Completion

1. The tense relationship between the United States and the Soviet Union began in the closing months of _____ .

2. The _____ was a program that provided broad economic aid to European states on the sole condition that they work together for their mutual benefit.

3. The murder of _____ was an early sign of communist intentions in eastern Europe.

4. The 1955 formation of the _____ as an eastern bloc military alliance demonstrated the extent of Cold War politics in Europe.

5. As early as 1917 the British government in issuing the _____ favored the establishment of a Jewish homeland in Palestine.

6. It would appear that the U.S. involvement in the early 1950s Korean conflict was interpreted by American policy makers as a success for the concept known as _____ .

7. The erection of the Berlin Wall occurred during the American presidency of _____ .

8. The defeat of the French forces in the battle of _____ effectively ended France's involvement in Indochina.

9. President Richard Nixon's policy aimed at the gradual withdrawal of American combat forces from Vietnam was known as _____ .

10. Under the policy of _____ , Gorbachev proposed major economic and political reforms of the various centralized economic ministries.

For Further Consideration

1. In your opinion, how did the American response to and policy development in respect to the Korean "police action" of 1950–1953 relate to later U.S. involvement in Vietnam?

2. Discuss the economic experiments sponsored under Nikita Khrushchev's leadership of the Soviet Union. Did these policies have a later effect? If so, discuss their implications in detail.

3. Describe the course of events in the post-World War II rivalry between the United States and the Soviet Union. Cite the significant examples of this superpower competition. What in your view led to the end of the Cold War?

4. What were the origins of the Indochina conflict? Discuss the motivations of the major participants in that area's troubles over the thirty-year period beginning in 1945. Try to characterize the positions of each of the following countries: France, Russia, China, United States, South Vietnam, North Vietnam.

5. Discuss the leadership of Gorbachev in the Soviet Union. Do you think that the same events would have occurred in the Soviet Union had he remained in power? Why or why not? What do you think the relationship between the United States and the former Soviet Union would be like if Gorbachev was still leader?

Answers

Multiple-Choice

		Text page
1.	D	595
2.	B	595
3.	D	599
4.	C	600
5.	C	601
6.	C	606
7.	D	607
8.	A	607-608
9.	D	609
10.	D	614

True/False

1.	F	595
2.	T	595
3.	F	595
4.	F	600
5.	T	601-602
6.	T	604
7.	T	604
8.	F	604
9.	T	605
10.	F	605

Completion

1.	World War II	594
2.	Marshall Plan	595
3.	Jan Masaryk	596
4.	Warsaw Pact	596
5.	Balfour Declaration	597
6.	containment	599
7.	John F. Kennedy	601
8.	Dien Bien Phu	603
9.	*Vietnamization*	604
10.	perestroika	608-609